THE WO **S**

D0402214

Pakistan

**Other Books in the
World's Hot Spots series:**

Afghanistan
Iraq
The Palestinians and the Disputed Territories
Saudi Arabia

THE WORLD'S H🔥T SPOTS

Pakistan

Adrian Sinkler, *Book Editor*

Daniel Leone, *President*
Bonnie Szumski, *Publisher*
Scott Barbour, *Managing Editor*

**GREENHAVEN
PRESS®**

THOMSON
™
GALE

San Diego • Detroit • New York • San Francisco • Cleveland
New Haven, Conn. • Waterville, Maine • London • Munich

THOMSON

------------✳------------ ™

GALE

LIBRARY OF CONGRESS CATALOGING-IN-PUBLICATION DATA
Pakistan / Adrian Sinkler, book editor.
p. cm. — (The world's hot spots)
Includes bibliographical references and index.
ISBN 0-7377-1459-X (pbk. : alk. paper) — ISBN 0-7377-1458-1 (lib. : alk. paper)
1. Pakistan—History. I. Sinkler, Adrian. II. Series.
DS384 .P323 2003
954.91—dc21   2002032213

 **CONTENTS**

went to war over Kashmir, the status of which remains a contested issue and an almost constant source of conflict, and sometimes war, between the two countries.

2. Pakistan's Position on Nuclear Proliferation in South Asia
In May 1998, Pakistan successfully tested its first nuclear weapons in response to similar tests conducted by its archrival India. By demonstrating their nuclear capabilities, India and Pakistan raised the stakes in their conflict over Kashmir.

3. The Social Costs of Nuclear Proliferation
In order to develop their nuclear programs, India and Pakistan committed many of their scarce resources to national defense instead of other social programs. This arms race between India and Pakistan placed heavy burdens on the citizens of both countries, especially in the areas of public health, education, and economic growth.

4. The Persistence of the Indo-Pakistani Conflict
A terrorist attack on the Indian Parliament building in December 2001 demonstrated that American and British mediation can reduce tensions in South Asia, but it also demonstrated that there is still a real danger of war between India and Pakistan.

5. An Argument for Kashmiri Independence
One of the potential solutions to the conflict between India and Pakistan is to grant Kashmir its independence. Though the Indian and Pakistani governments would not support such a resolution, independence is increasingly popular among Kashmiris themselves.

Chapter 3: Pakistan and the War on Terror
1. Pakistan Must Join the War on Terror
Despite the potential for backlash from radical Islamic

groups, President Pervez Musharraf announced that Pakistan would support the American war effort in Afghanistan on September 19, 2001.

they had outlived their strategic importance. Pakistan's leaders risked suffering the same fate as previous American and British clients in the Third World when they agreed to join the American-led War on Terror.

◈ FOREWORD

The American Heritage Dictionary defines the term *hot spot* as "an area in which there is dangerous unrest or hostile action." Though it is probably true that almost any conceivable "area" contains potentially "dangerous unrest or hostile action," there are certain countries in the world especially susceptible to conflict that threatens the lives of noncombatants on a regular basis. After the events of September 11, 2001, the consequences of this particular kind of conflict and the importance of the countries, regions, or groups that produce it are even more relevant for all concerned public policy makers, citizens, and students. Perhaps now more than ever, the violence and instability that engulfs the world's hot spots truly has a global reach and demands the attention of the entire international community.

The scope of problems caused by regional conflicts is evident in the extent to which international policy makers have begun to assert themselves in efforts to reduce the tension and violence that threatens innocent lives around the globe. The U.S. Congress, for example, recently addressed the issue of economic stability in Pakistan by considering a trading bill to encourage growth in the Pakistani textile industry. The efforts of some congresspeople to improve the economic conditions in Pakistan through trade with the United States was more than an effort to address a potential economic cause of the instability engulfing Pakistani society. It was also an acknowledgment that domestic issues in Pakistan are connected to domestic political issues in the United States. Without a concerted effort by policy makers in the United States, or any other country for that matter, it is quite possible that the violence and instability that shatters the lives of Pakistanis will not only continue, but will also worsen and threaten the stability and prosperity of other regions.

Recent international efforts to reach a peaceful settlement of the Israeli-Palestinian conflict also demonstrate how peace and stability in the Middle East is not just a regional issue. The toll on Palestinian and Israeli lives is easy to see through the suicide bombings and rocket attacks in Israeli cities and in the occupied territories of the West Bank and Gaza. What is, perhaps, not as evident is the extent to which this conflict involves the rest of the world. Saudi Arabia and Iran, for instance, have long been at odds and have attempted to gain control of the conflict by supporting competing organizations dedicated to a Palestinian state. These groups have often used Saudi and Iranian financial and political support to carry out violent attacks against Israeli civilians and military installations. Of course, the issue goes far beyond a struggle between two regional powers to gain control of the region's most visible issue. Many analysts and leaders have also argued that the West's military and political support of Israel is one of the leading factors that motivated al-Qaeda's September 11 attacks on New York and Washington, D.C. In many ways, this regional conflict is an international affair that will require international solutions.

The World's Hot Spots series is intended to meet the demand for information and discussion among young adults and students who would like to better understand the areas embroiled in conflicts that contribute to catastrophic events like those of September 11. Each volume of The World's Hot Spots is an anthology of primary and secondary documents that provides historical background to the conflict, or conflicts, under examination. The books also provide students with a wide range of opinions from world leaders, activists, and professional writers concerning the root causes and potential solutions to the problems facing the countries covered in this series. In addition, extensive research tools such as an annotated table of contents, bibliography, and glossaries of terms and important figures provide readers a foundation from which they can build their knowledge of some of the world's most pressing issues. The information and opinions presented in The World's Hot Spots series will give students some of the tools they will need to become active participants in the ongoing dialogue concerning the globe's most volatile regions.

🔥 INTRODUCTION

I n late 1998, four high-level Pakistani military officials met to discuss plans for an operation in the mountainous terrain around the town of Kargil, which lies on the Indian side of the Line of Control (LoC) in the disputed state of Kashmir. The plans were made in spite of recent diplomatic efforts to ease longtime tensions between India and Pakistan and involved placing troops in an area that the Indian army usually evacuated during the harsh mountain winters. In March 1999, Chief of Army Staff General Pervez Musharraf ordered about a thousand Pakistani soldiers, who were aided by some Kashmiri guerrillas, into the vacated Dras region around Kargil. When Indian forces returned to their posts in May 1999, they met Pakistani troops who fired on them and inflicted heavy casualties.

At the time of the Kargil offensive, many analysts worried that the Pakistani operation would lead to a full-scale war between the two South Asian rivals. The consequences of such a war were especially troubling because both India and Pakistan possessed nuclear weapons that could have been deployed and detonated at their targets in a matter of minutes. Fearing the ramifications of conflict between nuclear-armed states, many governments around the world, including the Clinton administration in the United States, pressured Pakistan to withdraw its forces from the Indian side of the LoC. Under international pressure, Prime Minister Nawaz Sharif ordered the withdrawal of Pakistani troops and attempted to replace some of the military officers who planned and executed the Kargil offensive. On October 12, 1999, the military officers revolted against Sharif's decision, sending him into exile and, in a bloodless coup, installing General Musharraf as the chief executive of Pakistan.

The events surrounding the Kargil offensive are indicative of two major issues that trouble analysts and policy makers concerned with contemporary affairs in Pakistan. The first is Pakistan's turbulent relationship with India, which has resulted in three major wars and countless other small skirmishes and, since 1998, has had the potential to produce the world's first full-scale nuclear war. Invariably, each of the past confrontations between India and Pakistan was linked to Kashmir, an area that both countries have fought to control since they gained their independence from Britain in 1947.

The second major issue illustrated by the Kargil incident is the tur-

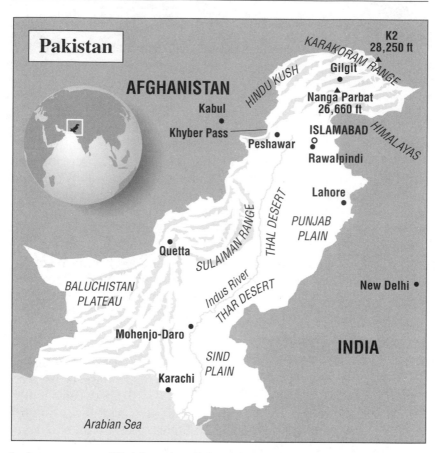

bulent nature of Pakistani politics, which includes factions with a propensity to use violence as a mechanism to advance their goals. Many of these groups consist of soldiers and officers in the military, an institution that many scholars claim is the most powerful in Pakistan, but other groups, many of which advocate a strict interpretation of Islamic law, also demonstrate a tendency to use violence as a means to achieve their political aims. In the past, the military encouraged, or supported, the behavior of these groups because their goals coincided with those of military leaders or because the military indirectly benefited from the instability that these groups caused. Regardless of the reasons for the military support, the political turmoil Pakistan experienced because of it significantly harmed the welfare of its citizenry and threatened the peace and stability of South Asia throughout the 1980s and 1990s.

Pakistan's relations with India and the unstable nature of its internal politics have long been a concern, but these issues took on even greater importance after the terrorist attacks in New York and

Washington, D.C., on September 11, 2001. The added importance of Pakistan in the wake of these attacks is in part a function of geography. Pakistan borders Afghanistan, which is where the American effort to combat terrorism began. However, the importance of Pakistan in the context of the War on Terror has as much to do with its historical development as an independent nation as it does with its location. As is true of every other country in the world, Pakistan's position on the contemporary world stage is not just a product of contemporary events.

Background on the Conflict with India

The current conflict between India and Pakistan is directly linked to the period of British rule, which officially began in 1858. The Indian subcontinent consists of numerous ethnic and religious groups, and during the period of the British Raj, or empire, these groups were either ruled directly by the British government or ruled by semiautonomous princes. The princes were the leading political authority in their areas of control, known as princely states or protectorates, but they were still subordinate to the British monarch. In exchange for authority over matters within their princely states, the princes paid a tribute to the British government and granted it supremacy in matters of trade and foreign affairs. By the early twentieth century, this mixed system of administration began to create tensions between the central government of British India and the princes, who felt that their treaty rights were unduly restricted.

In addition to the tension between the princely states and the central government, a movement to gain more local autonomy for Indians who lived in the areas under direct British control began in the late nineteenth century. In 1885, a group of Indian intellectuals and political leaders formed the Indian National Congress, a political party intended to promote the interests of the native inhabitants of British India. Some members in the congress argued that these interests could be protected only if India gained full independence from the British. Although most members of the Indian National Congress agreed with the goal of achieving more local autonomy, they did not all agree on the issue of independence, which created several divisions between radical and moderate factions within the party. One of the divisions that proved to have a lasting effect on the future of South Asia was the division between the two major religious groups in British India: Hindus and Muslims.

Conflicts between Hindus and Muslims in South Asia had begun in the seventh century A.D., when the first Arab invaders brought Islam to the region, but the political conflict that ultimately led to the division of British India began in 1906. At the time, Muslim political and religious leaders in India feared the growing power of the Hindu-dominated Indian National Congress and attempted to offset its power by forming their own political party, the All-India Muslim League. The original intent of the Muslim League was to protect the interests of the Muslim minority within a united British India, but it eventually became the driving force behind the movement for a separate Muslim country in South Asia.

The events that convinced Muslim leaders in India to press for a separate Muslim state took place in the years following the First World War, from which Britain and its allies emerged victorious after Germany signed the Treaty of Versailles in 1919. One of the conditions of peace gave the British and their French allies control over the territories that formerly belonged to the Ottoman Empire, which fought with Germany during the war. The Ottoman Empire contained vast portions of the Middle East and North Africa and was regarded as the political center of the Muslim world prior to its defeat in World War I. Once the British and the French had seized control of Ottoman territory, they announced their intent to divide it into smaller units and strip the Ottoman caliph—the earthly political leader of the Muslims—of his power. Indian Muslims vehemently opposed this policy, fearing that a loss of political power for Muslims in the Middle East would lessen their influence in India, not only in relation to the British but to the Hindu majority as well.

In response to British policy in the Middle East, Indian Muslims organized a political movement, known as the Khilafat movement (1919–1924), which sought to protect the integrity of the Ottoman Empire and the rights of Muslims in British India. Despite the efforts of the leading Indian nationalist, Mohandas Gandhi, to unite the Khilafat movement with his noncooperation movement into a larger coalition for Indian independence, the more radical members of the All-India Muslim League and the Khilafat movement began to agitate the Muslim population in India, urging it to resist the demands of non-Muslims. The campaign of agitation by radical Muslim leaders eventually contributed to the Mapilla rebellion of 1921, which quickly turned into a communal riot between Muslim peasants and their Hindu landlords in the southwestern province of Malabar.

Communal rioting between Hindus and Muslims became more common after the revolt in Malabar and was one of several factors that prompted some Muslim leaders to distance themselves from the national movement for Indian independence. The most important of these leaders was Mohammed Ali Jinnah, a lawyer who began his political career in 1906 when he joined the Indian National Congress.

In 1913, Jinnah also became a member of the All-India Muslim League, a decision that created a dilemma for him once disagreements between Hindus and Muslims about the future of India began to surface. Believing he had to make a choice between the two political parties, Jinnah resigned his post with the Indian National Congress in 1919 and devoted the rest of his political career to the Muslim League and the protection of Muslim rights in India.

Jinnah did not advocate the idea of a separate Muslim state at first, but later in his career, for reasons that are difficult to determine, he reached the conclusion that a united India after independence would threaten Muslim interests and autonomy. On March 23, 1940, Jinnah addressed the All-India Muslim League and urged its members to adopt the Lahore Resolution, which called for the establishment of an independent Muslim state. A few days later, the league voted in favor of the resolution, making the demand for an independent Muslim country in South Asia an official goal of some of the most prominent Indian Muslims.

The British and the Indian National Congress did not initially receive the idea of Muslim independence with much enthusiasm; in fact, the idea was also not very popular among the majority of Indian Muslims. Despite the resistance it faced, the All-India Muslim League managed to organize widespread support for the partition of India among a significant number of Muslims by the early 1940s. The momentum that the "Pakistan movement" gained during this period was due in large part to the tireless efforts and political skill of Jinnah, who convinced the British and the Indian National Congress to take the idea of Muslim independence seriously.

As the Indian independence and Muslim nationalist movements gained strength in the 1930s and 1940s, Britain attempted to restore order and reassert its control of India by inducing the semiautonomous princely states to join a new Indian federation in which they would exchange some of their internal sovereignty for representation in a new national assembly. Much to the disappointment of the British, the princes refused the plan outlined by the Government of India Act of 1935, signaling the beginning of the end for Britain's Indian Empire. When Britain entered World War II in September 1939, it faced the difficult and expensive task of balancing an international war effort with the administration of a vast colony in the midst of serious political turmoil. It was a task that eventually became too costly.

Under pressure from its American allies and its Indian subjects, Britain finally agreed to grant independence to India following World War II, but it was not clear that Britain intended to divide the Indian subcontinent after the war. In fact, the British made one last attempt to keep India unified after the war ended with its Cabinet Mission Plan of 1946. The plan would have divided India into three different regions—two of which would have been Muslim majority regions— and tied them together in a loose federation from which each region could have voted to secede after a fifteen-year period.

Indian National Congress president Jawaharlal Nehru initially backed the plan, but he reserved the right for the congress to block the secession of either of the Muslim regions if they attempted to leave the proposed federation. Nehru's declaration convinced the Muslim League that any union with a Hindu majority would threaten Muslim autonomy; the Muslim League formally rejected the Cabinet Mission Plan in the summer of 1946. Lacking any clear alternative, Britain granted independence to the people of its South Asian Empire on August 14, 1947, dividing them between the Muslim state of Pakistan and the nominally secular state of India.

The partition of India followed the territorial prescriptions of the Cabinet Mission Plan of 1946, ceding the Muslim majority areas in the northwest and the northeast to Pakistan and giving the remaining territory to India. The princes of the semiautonomous protectorates, on the other hand, were given the option of independence or joining either of the two new countries provided they shared a border with the country to which they acceded. This arrangement produced serious complications, igniting flames of communal violence and mutual distrust between Hindus and Muslims throughout India, especially in the princely state of Kashmir.

Kashmir's location between Pakistan and India, and its fertile Vale valley, made it a desirable acquisition for both of the new countries in South Asia. Unfortunately, the internal political condition of Kashmir did not lend itself to an easy resolution of the accession issue. Violence between Hindus and Muslims in the neighboring state of Punjab spread to Kashmir in the summer of 1947, prompting Kashmir's Hindu prince to request assistance from India to restore order. The prince's decision to involve Indian forces in the conflict deeply upset the majority Muslim population in Kashmir and contributed to more communal rioting and confrontations with the Indian army. Sensing an opportunity to win Kashmir by force, Pakistani prime minister Liaquat Ali Khan in 1947 ordered Pakistani troops to intervene and protect the Muslim population. Thus began the first of three wars between India and Pakistan, a war that ended in a stalemate and a cease-fire agreement that divided Kashmir into Pakistani and Indian areas of control.

After sixteen years of relative peace, war broke out again in 1965

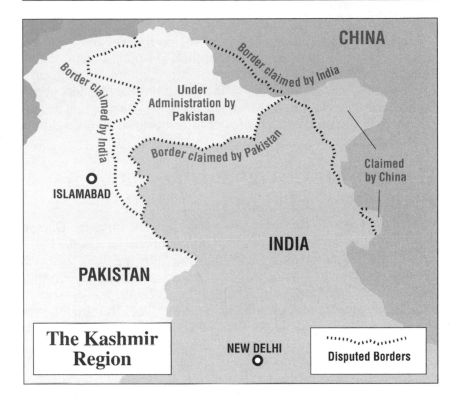

CHINA

Border claimed by India

Under
Administration by
Pakistan

Border claimed by Pakistan

Claimed
by China

Border claimed by India

ISLAMABAD

INDIA

PAKISTAN

The Kashmir
Region

NEW DELHI

Disputed Borders

when Pakistan armed and trained thousands of mujahideen, or Muslim freedom fighters, and sent them into Indian-Occupied Kashmir (IOK). The operation was designed to give the impression that Kashmiris were in open revolt against Indian rule, but once the Indian government discovered that the mujahideen were backed by the Pakistani military, it responded by sending troops into the southern part of Pakistan near the port city of Lahore. On the morning of September 6, 1965, war broke out between India and Pakistan, but once again, hostilities ended in a stalemate seventeen days later.

Unlike the first two wars, the war of 1971 did not end in a standoff and did not begin in Kashmir. Hostilities broke out in East Pakistan, where the majority Bengali population was pressing for independence, eventually gaining it and forming the state of Bangladesh with the help of the Indian army. A few days later, fighting again spread to Kashmir, where India pushed Pakistani troops behind the 1948 cease-fire line. When the fighting ended on December 21, 1971, Pakistan was cut in half and had been badly beaten in Kashmir. The war was an embarrassment to Pakistani political and military leaders, who knew that their hopes of being treated as political and military equals with India were diminishing.

Pakistan's fear of becoming a "minimal" power in South Asia was heightened by India's first nuclear explosion in 1974 and by an aggressive Indian military exercise near the Pakistani border in 1986. In order to offset India's military advantage and protect Pakistan's interests in Kashmir, Pakistani military and political leaders began making preparations for their own nuclear weapons program and attempting to influence the politics of their northwestern neighbors in Afghanistan.

Covert War in Afghanistan and Instability in Pakistan

The border between Pakistan and Afghanistan, known as the Durand Line, cuts through the heart of the traditional homeland of the Pashtuns, nomadic people who have a reputation for being fierce warriors. During the period of British rule in India, the Northwest Frontier Province, which is principally inhabited by Pashtuns, was the one region in the British Indian Empire that the royal armies could not completely subdue. When the British left in 1947, the Northwest Frontier Province became a part of Pakistan and proved to be just as difficult for its new rulers as it was for the British.

The main source of difficulty in the northwest was ethnic separatism among the Pashtuns, who at different times threatened to secede from Pakistan. The secessionist sentiments of Pashtuns in Pakistan reached a crescendo in the period following Pakistani independence when the Afghan government of King Nadir Shah refused to accept the Durand Line as the legal border between Pakistan and Afghanistan. The king, along with his prime minister Muhammad Daud, claimed the line was illegitimate, largely because he felt it was a remnant of British imperialism that unfairly divided the Pashtun population. His claim found many sympathizers among Pakistani Pashtuns and successive Afghan governments that argued in favor of redrawing the border between Afghanistan and Pakistan in order to create a homeland for the Pashtuns. Some Afghan political leaders called for the full incorporation of the Northwest Frontier Province into Afghanistan; others indicated they would accept a second scenario that involved creating a new, independent country for the Pashtuns. Both of these scenarios would force Pakistan to cede much of its northwestern territory, a proposition that continues to be unacceptable from the Pakistani perspective.

The Afghan demands for a Pashtun homeland, or Pashtunistan, contributed to the tense relationship between Pakistan and Afghanistan in the years following 1947, but internal political problems in

Pakistan often created tension as well. One instance of internal tur-moil prompted Prime Minister Zulfikar Ali Bhutto to outlaw a Pash-tun separatist group in 1973 on the pretext that it was working with the Afghan government to challenge the sovereignty of Pakistan in the Northwest Frontier Province. Ethnic separatism among Pashtuns in the northwest became even more troubling to Pakistanis after the 1971 war with India. Pakistani leaders worried that a hostile gov-ernment in Afghanistan could successfully augment and support eth-nic separatism in Pakistan, allowing India to take advantage of the internal instability and move into the remainder of Pakistan-Occupied Kashmir (POK) and, perhaps, even into Pakistan itself.

Surrounded by hostile neighbors, Pakistan's political and military leaders attempted to improve their strategic position in the region by supporting dissidents that resisted the incumbent government in Af-ghanistan. This approach, known as "strategic depth," began in the early 1970s and was intended to encourage a political change in Af-ghanistan and install a government more sympathetic to the wishes of Pakistan's political leadership. Pakistani authorities believed that a friendly regime in Afghanistan would stem the tide of ethnic sep-aratism in Pakistan and serve as a check on their militarily superior enemy, India. Among other things, Pakistan's strategy involved pro-viding arms and tactical support to small guerrilla groups that oper-ated in Afghanistan and, if necessary, retreated into Pakistan for cover. The groups Pakistan supported were, more often than not, the most radical factions of Afghan society that professed a strict inter-pretation of the Koran (the Muslim holy book) and advocated an Is-lamic state in Afghanistan.

The dynamics of Pakistan's strategic depth policy drastically changed in 1979, when the Soviet Union invaded Afghanistan in sup-port of a Communist government that had come to power through a coup in 1978. Pakistan's leaders again feared the intentions of an overwhelmingly superior military power and, with the aid of the United States, intensified their support for Afghan dissidents. The Pakistani Inter-Services Intelligence (ISI), the Pakistani equivalent of America's CIA, took direct control of operations in Afghanistan, funneling American military aid to the mujahideen, providing tacti-cal assistance and training, and coordinating Afghan refugee camps inside Pakistan.

As they did before the Soviet invasion of Afghanistan, and for most of the same reasons, Pakistani leaders tended to favor the most radical groups within the mujahideen. Mohammad Zia-ul-Haq, Pak-istan's chief executive after gaining power in 1977 through a mili-tary coup, believed that supporting radical Islamic groups in Afghanistan would quiet the ethnic separatist movement in the frontier regions of Pakistan. He also believed that an Islamic state in Afghanistan would serve as an extension of the Pakistani army, which would be capable of coming to the aid of its Muslim brothers to the south should a conflict with India threaten Pakistan or its interests in Kashmir.

The group most favored by the ISI was the Hezb-i-Islami, an opponent of the Afghan government that conducted many of its operations from bases inside Pakistan. The military regime of Zia-ul-Haq chose this group because it shared the goal of an Islamic state in Afghanistan and because it had close ties to a radical Islamic group in Pakistan, the Jamaat-i-Islami, which ardently backed Zia's pan-Islamic platform. These radical groups gained strength throughout the Soviet war with the support of the Pakistani military and the American CIA, as well as radical Islamic groups in the Middle East. Muslims from all over the world came to Afghanistan and Pakistan to join the jihad, or holy war, against the Soviets, and many of them brought with them a strict version of Islam that left little room for non-Muslim influences on Islamic societies.

After the Soviets withdrew from Afghanistan in February 1989, recently elected Pakistani prime minister Benazir Bhutto attempted to reform Pakistan's policy of supporting radical Islamic groups in Afghanistan. The prime minister dismissed the director general of the Inter-Services Intelligence and advocated a negotiated settlement in Afghanistan that would have produced a broad-based government made of different factions of the Afghan mujahideen and more moderate groups in Afghan society. Unfortunately for Bhutto, the relationship between the military and radical Islamic groups was difficult to break, and the ISI strongly resisted her efforts to reform the military and change Pakistan's policy in Afghanistan.

Despite the efforts of moderate political leaders to institute reform, Pakistani military and intelligence officials continued their support for the radical Islamic factions inside Afghanistan and continued to develop a close relationship with radical groups in Pakistan well into the 1990s. One of the key elements of Pakistan's support for radical Muslims in Afghanistan was the promulgation of *madrasas*, or religious schools, throughout the Northwest Frontier Province. These schools served as the training ground for a group of young Muslim students known as the Taliban, which launched a military offensive in Afghanistan in the summer of 1995. With the aid of Pakistani military and intelligence officials, the Taliban conquered most of Afghanistan by early 1996 and instituted a strict Islamic political regime in which men were required to grow beards, women were forbidden from working, and girls were banned from schools, among other measures.

The consequences of Pakistan's strategic depth policy in Afghanistan included not only the emergence of a radical Islamic regime in Afghanistan but also a rise in Islamic fundamentalism within Pakistan. Radical groups like the Jamaat-i-Islami grew in strength throughout the 1990s, as did the Pakistani *madrasas* that continued to train young Muslims for an ongoing jihad against non-Muslim cultures. Some of the young students became guerrillas in Indian-Occupied Kashmir with the support of military leaders, complicating an already tense relationship between the nuclear-armed governments of India and Pakistan. Others became involved in terrorist organizations in the Middle East and other regions throughout the world, inflicting damage on both civilian and military targets. For Pakistanis, the rise of radical Islamic groups made it difficult for moderate leaders to share political power, let alone reform Pakistani society and put it on a path toward peace and prosperity.

Musharraf's Dilemma: Pakistan After September 11, 2001

Pervez Musharraf became the fourth president in the history of Pakistan to gain power through a military coup on October 12, 1999. Like his predecessors, Musharraf inherited a tense relationship with India and harbored a deep commitment to the Kashmir issue. The depth of his commitment to Kashmir manifested itself during the Kargil offensive in the spring of 1999, when he ordered Pakistani troops to engage the Indian army despite the inherent risks of such an operation, risks that included the nuclear annihilation of Pakistan's major cities and the death of thousands of Pakistani civilians. Early in his tenure, Musharraf also continued the dubious tradition of using radical Islamic groups to advance his goals in Kashmir and Afghanistan despite the international condemnation he received for doing so.

Events that occurred before he came to power determined the conditions Musharraf inherited in Pakistan, and, to a large degree, past events affected the strategies he used to gain and maintain political power. However, events that occurred during his second year in office will probably have the most lasting effect on his legacy as a leader in world politics. On September 11, 2001, nineteen Saudi-born men attacked the World Trade Center in New York and the Pentagon in Washington, D.C., with commercial airliners. The magnitude of the attacks drastically changed the worldviews of pundits and policy makers worldwide, but there are few places in the world where the change in international politics had a greater impact than in Pakistan.

After the attacks on New York and Washington, Musharraf was forced to make a difficult choice: to join the American-led war effort in Afghanistan or face the potentially drastic consequences of refusing to cooperate. Joining the war meant reversing Pakistan's support of radical Islamic groups and, at least in the short term, accepting the status quo in Kashmir. Refusing to cooperate with the American-led war effort meant facing the superior military power of the United States and perhaps losing Kashmir to India in the process. Musharraf chose to cooperate with the United States, but the consequences of his decision, as sound as it may have been, are the reason that Pakistan remains one of the world's hot spots.

Groups that the Pakistani military once supported became enemies of the state after Musharraf agreed to assist the United States in the War on Terror. These groups strongly resisted Musharraf's decision, and they have the potential to destabilize Pakistan by placing a more radical leader in power. The consequences of such a development are especially troubling given Pakistan's history of animosity toward India, which gained the upper hand in the Kashmir issue in the wake of the terrorist attacks on the United States. No longer can Pakistan support Kashmiri guerrillas, who are now considered terrorists, and no longer can it hope to resolve the issue with covert military operations. The only legitimate options open to Pakistan after September 11 are to wait for a peaceful settlement of the Kashmir issue, brokered by international actors, or to directly confront India. The first option could lead to a revolt in Pakistan spearheaded by militant Islamic groups; the second could end in a nuclear war.

The forces unleashed by the partition of British India in 1947 combined with the acts of nineteen men on September 11, 2001, make the outcome of the political drama in Pakistan a crucial consideration for millions of people. If Pakistan successfully navigates the troubled waters on which it sails, it will enhance the prospects for peace and positive social change in South Asia. If Pakistan fails to find a solution to its internal problems, the consequences of its failure could be devastating. How will the political drama in Pakistan end, and what, if anything, can be done to ensure a positive outcome? These are among the many questions that the authors selected for this volume attempt to answer.

CHAPTER 1

The Roots of Conflict

The Partition of British India

By Francis Robinson

Francis Robinson is professor of the history of South Asia and is the vice principal of Royal Holloway at the University of London, where he has researched the historical development of Islam in South Asia since 1993. In this selection, Robinson describes the rise of Muslim and Hindu religious revivalism in the mid–nineteenth and early twentieth centuries and the role of religious and political leaders, such as Saiyid Ahmad Khan and Muhammad Iqbal, in fomenting the rise of Muslim separatist thought. These developments are among the many factors that contributed to the conflict that led to the division of British India into Hindu and Muslim states as well as the tremendous communal violence that would follow.

The partition of India at independence in 1947 into the sovereign states of India and Pakistan is one of the more important events of twentieth-century world history. It was a shameful end to the most important project in Britain's imperial enterprise. More important, it was a tragic experience for the hundreds of thousands of Hindus, Sikhs and Muslims who were killed in the communal slaughter which accompanied the process and for the nearly 15 million who were made refugees. Over the past fifty years India and Pakistan have been in a state of constant hostility, fighting three wars in 1947–48, 1963 and 1971, and during the last decade fighting low-intensity wars over Kashmir and the drawing of boundaries in the high Himalayas.

Approaches to partition depend very much on where the individual is situated. For Indians, in the classic nationalist interpretation, partition was the logical outcome of Britain's policies of dividing and ruling. For Pakistanis it was their founding moment, the glorious outcome of the struggle of Muslims to have their separate identity recognised by both the British and the Indian nationalist movement. For the Bangladeshis, it was a false dawn, but arguably a necessary prelude to their achievement of their own nation state in 1971. For the British it was a regrettable necessity. They did not have the power to impose a solution on their Indian empire which left it unified; partition came to be the only way in which they could extract themselves from a commitment which they could no longer afford. . . .

Understanding Muslim Separatism

In any explanation of 'Muslim separatism' the following elements should play a part. Some weight should be given to Islamic values. There is a tendency for some Muslims to organise on a community basis whenever they go into politics. At the level of religious belief there are powerful drives for communal action. God told Muslims through the Prophet Mohammad that they were the 'best community raised up for mankind'. God revealed to Muslims the best way to live if they hoped for salvation, and that involved living within the community and being subject to its law. The idea of community action for community ends has a seductive resonance. However, for a good number of Muslims the idea of community was more a rhetorical flourish than a psychological fact.

Weight should certainly be given to Muslim revivalism. From the beginning of the nineteenth century Indian Muslims, in common with Muslims elsewhere in the world, were in the grip of various movements of revival and reform. These came to intersect with the problems of coping with the meaning of Western power and Western knowledge. There was considerable cultural and intellectual ferment as Muslims in different social and intellectual situations fashioned ways forward. Various movements were founded—those of the Deobandis, Barelvis, Ahmadis, Jamaati-Islamis and Tablighi-Jamaatis— which have come to have worldwide significance. In India they tended to draw firmer distinctions between Muslim practice and that of the Hindu world around them; the outcome was to sharpen the Muslim sense of identity.

From a political point of view the most important part of this process was the attempt of the leading intellectual, Saiyid Ahmad Khan, to build a bridge between Islamic learning and Western science on the one hand, and the Muslim landed and professional classes and British rule on the other. This effort had its institutional focus in the Cambridge-style college which the Saiyid founded in 1877 in the form of the Mohammadan Anglo-Oriental College at Aligarh, some ninety miles from Delhi. The students and supporters of this college were to play the leading role in carrying forward the cause of Muslim separatism.

The Importance of Hindu Revivalism

But it was not just Islam which was challenged by Western power and knowledge: so was Hinduism, the faith of the great majority of Indians. Hindus also experienced a cultural and intellectual ferment, and came to have a sharper sense of their identity. Some hailed British rule for supplanting 'Muslim tyranny'. Muslims were accused of robbing Hindus of religion, wealth and women. They were the outsiders in India, not Hindustanis. The relics of Muslim power, such as mosques in Hindu holy places, were 'wounds in the heart'. In northern India Hindus and Muslims began to rub up against each other more abrasively, particularly as the former demanded an end to the slaughter of cows (cheap food for Muslims but holy for Hindus) and the replacement of the Persian script in government by the Hindu Nagri script. The presence of Hindu revivalists tended to inhibit the nationalist movement when it sought compromise with the Muslim League. . . .

That the British understood Indian society in terms of its religious divisions was always an important prop of the nationalist accusation that Indians were divided, and India ultimately divided, by British policies of divide and rule. There is a smidgeon of truth in these accusations, although British policies are better understood as a series of pragmatic responses to a changing political environment rather than a conscious policy to divide. 'Nothing', declared one leading administrator in the late nineteenth century, 'could be more opposed to the policy and universal practice of our government in India than the old maxim of divide and rule . . .'.

The Establishment of Aligarh College and the Muslim League

At this time the British felt Muslims to be the greatest threat to their rule. They had failed to reconcile the former rulers of India to their government; the Mutiny uprising of 1857 was seen to confirm this. In 1870 they decided that the safety of the Raj demanded that they find ways of attaching powerful Muslims to their side. This policy was developed just at the time that Saiyid Ahmad Khan was striving to reconcile his co-religionists to Western knowledge and British rule. His initiatives received much official encouragement. Arguably his Aligarh College would never have been founded, and may not have survived, but for government support which ranged from land made available at derisory rates to personal donations from viceroys. His All-India Muslim Educational Conference, which from 1886 drew

Muslims together from all over India for the first time, operated within a framework of government approval. He himself was given the most unusual distinction, for an Indian at the time, of being knighted.

Aligarh College and the Educational Conference were the institutional bases on which the All-India Muslim League, the spearhead of Muslim separatism, was founded in 1906. The first office of the League was at Aligarh; its first secretary was the College secretary. The League's first major campaign was to demand separate electorates for Muslims, and extra representation in those areas in which they were 'politically important' such as the United Provinces (UP), in the new legislative councils which Viceroy Minto and Secretary of State Morley were developing for India. With some misgivings the British were persuaded and these privileges were granted in the Council reforms of 1909. Thus a separate Muslim identity was enshrined in India's growing framework of electoral politics. When in 1919 and 1935 the franchise was extended and further powers were devolved, separate electorates were continued and the principle of Muslim separateness confirmed.

The Pakistan Movement Gains Momentum

Many factors—Islamic values, religious revivalism, British understandings of India and British techniques of rule—helped to establish an important step along the road towards India's partition. We should note, however, that such roads rarely run straight and that different groups of Muslims found the platform suiting their interests at different times. Initially supporters were the landed and government service classes, mainly from the UP, the supporters of Saiyid Ahmad Khan. By the First World War they were increasingly young professional men from the same province—lawyers and newspaper editors. In the 1920s the platform was virtually deserted; Muslim landlords joined landlord parties, some young professionals joined the nationalist movement, others left politics altogether. Towards the end of the 1920s as further devolution of power came to be discussed, Muslims crowded back onto the platform again. But many soon lost interest when they found it to be dominated by a view of the future favouring Muslims of the Punjab.

In December 1930 the poet-philosopher, Muhammad Iqbal, sketched out this view when, as President of the Muslim League session at Allahabad, he proposed the creation of a Muslim state in the north-west of India. This subsequently inspired a Cambridge student, Rahmat Ali, to give it a name 'Pakistan' derived thus: 'P' stood for the Punjab, 'A' for Afghanistan or the North-West Frontier Province, 'K' for Kashmir, 'S' for Sind and 'tan' for Baluchistan. It translated as the 'land of the pure'. . . .

In 1937 the Muslim League did not appear to be a major player in Indian politics. By 1946, however, it most certainly was. In the general elections of that year it won over 90 per cent of the seats reserved for Muslims. Its President, Jinnah, now known as the Quaid-i-Azam (Great Leader), had the support of the vast majority of India's Muslims. Any explanation of the partition of India must be able to explain this transformation of the League's position.

One key factor was the impact of the Second World War. It meant that the British were eager to seek Muslim support, in part because half the Indian army was Muslim and in part because the nationalist movement was opposed to the war and any Indian involvement in it. The League had little political clout, yet it was the only serious All-India Muslim party, so the British turned to it. . . .

Note should also be taken of the drive of Muslims from the Muslim minority provinces to build the League. In their view, if the League was to be heard, and they were to have adequate protection at independence, they had to win the support of Muslims in the majority provinces, most particularly Bengal and the Punjab. Here the cultural leadership of the UP amongst Indian Muslims had some part to play: learned and holy men from its leading traditional academies toured schools and shrines in the majority provinces to raise support, so too did students from what was now called the Aligarh Muslim University. But the main factors in its success were the League's capacity first to present a vote for the League as one for economic betterment for the Bengal peasant, and second to persuade the Punjab landlords, who controlled most Muslim votes in their province, that a vote for the League would be willy-nilly a vote for their future master.

Finally, there was the outstanding leadership abilities of Jinnah. He was masterly as the builder of the League as a political organisation, masterly as a political strategist and without equal as a negotiator. Few liked him; few doubted his integrity; everyone respected him. 'Of all the statesmen I have known in my life—Clemenceau, Lloyd George, Churchill, Curzon, Mussolini, Mahatma Gandhi', declared the Aga Khan, 'Jinnah is the most remarkable'. . . .

The British Division of India

From this point partition became increasingly inevitable. There was deadlock and growing civil disorder. A Labour Government in Britain was keen to leave India as fast as possible; every extra day

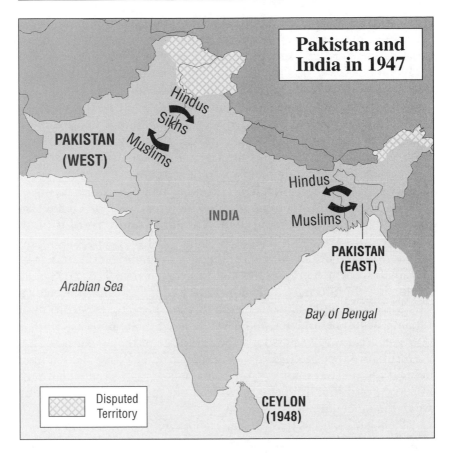

Pakistan and India in 1947

Hindus
Sikhs
Muslims

PAKISTAN
(WEST)

INDIA

Hindus

Muslims

PAKISTAN
(EAST)

Arabian Sea

Bay of Bengal

Disputed
Territory

CEYLON
(1948)

that British troops remained added to British debt. In February 1947 Mountbatten was sent out as Viceroy with a brief to pressure the politicians into agreement. Mountbatten quickly saw that Britain could only withdraw by transferring power not to one government, but to two. He also saw that it would not be possible to leave the large Hindu and Sikh minorities of the Punjab and the Hindu minority of Bengal under Muslim rule. The partition of India would also mean the partition of these provinces; thus the League had its two-nation theory played back against it. Jinnah was most unhappy to accept what he termed a 'truncated or mutilated and moth-eaten Pakistan', but eventually on June 3rd, 1947, he did, with a nod of the head. On August 14th, in Karachi, he was installed as Governor-General of the British dominion of Pakistan. Whatever his reservations, it seemed he had won a glorious victory.

There are some significant ironies in the making of partition. A common view would be that the Congress bitterly opposed the mutilation of Mother India. However, Congress did have a hand in the process itself. In the complete edition of his autobiography, *India Wins Freedom*, the Muslim member of the Congress high command, Abul Kalam Azad, makes it clear that of its other three members, Vallabhbhai Patel was positively in favour of partition before Mountbatten arrived, Nehru was quite quickly persuaded, and Gandhi accepted the inevitable. Patel and Nehru were keen to take over a strong central government and relatively weak provinces. Patel wanted strong central government to hold the new state together; Nehru was keen to put Soviet style five-year plans into effect. The Cabinet Mission plan patently did not supply strong central government.

A common view of Jinnah, on the other hand, sees him trying to resolve India's Muslim problem within the framework of a united India up to the late 1930s and then, from the Lahore resolution of March 1940, working for a separate state of Pakistan and fighting his way to triumph at partition. But the more recent interpretation of Ayesha Jalal, which is based on much fresh evidence, sees no change in Jinnah's long-term objective in 1940 and only a shift in strategy. The Lahore resolution was a bargaining card to gain recognition of Indian Muslim nationhood and the right to equal treatment at India's political centre; it was also a stick to bludgeon the Muslims of the majority provinces into supporting the League. When the Cabinet delegation made known its May proposals Jinnah's plans were realised; strong Muslim provinces need not feel concerned about a weak Indian centre.

When the Congress in effect rejected the proposals, Jinnah's plans were in tatters. In the remaining thirteen months leading up to independence, he worked to minimise the consequences of his defeat. Partition happened because, in the circumstances, the Congress leaders wanted it, not because Jinnah desired it.

The final irony was that Pakistan was built on a claim for a separate nationality for Muslims. Yet Pakistan's creation left one third of the subcontinent's Muslims in India, where they would have to subsume their Muslim identity within a greater Indian identity.

A Call for Muslim Independence

By Mohammed Ali Jinnah

Few people have inspired as much controversy among historians and pundits as Pakistan's first governor-general, Mohammed Ali Jinnah. The son of a wealthy merchant in Karachi, Jinnah studied law in Britain. He then returned to India, quickly making a name for himself as an advocate for the Bombay High Court. His political career began in 1906 when he joined the Indian National Congress, a political party devoted to Indian independence. He became a member of the All-India Muslim League in 1913.

Early in his career, Jinnah advocated that India be unified after achieving independence, but his views on the possibility of Hindu and Muslim unity gradually changed. In 1919, Jinnah resigned his position in the congress and devoted himself to the protection of Muslim interests in British India, which contained a substantial Hindu majority. In the following excerpt, Jinnah addresses the All-India Muslim League as its president in March 1940, arguing that Hindus and Muslims are incompatible and that each religious group should have its own country in South Asia.

L adies and Gentlemen, we are meeting to-day in our Session after months. The last session of the All-India Muslim League took place at Patna in December 1938. Since then many developments have taken place. I shall first shortly tell you what the All-India Muslim League had to face after the Patna Session of 1938.

Assessment of Developments Since 1938

You remember that one of the tasks, which was imposed on us and which is far from completed yet, was to organize Muslim Leagues all over India. We have made enormous progress during the last 15 months in this direction. I am glad to inform you that we have es-

Mohammed Ali Jinnah, "Presidential Address of Mr. M.A. Jinnah at the 27th Session of the All-India Muslim League, Lahore, March 1940," *Foundations of Pakistan, All-India Muslim League Documents: 1906–1947, Volume II (1924–1947)*, edited by Syed Sharifuddin Pirzada. Karachi: National Publishing House, Ltd., 1970. Copyright © 1970 by National Publishing House, Ltd. Reproduced by permission of the literary estate of Mohammed Ali Jinnah.

tablished Provincial Leagues in every Province. The next point is that in every by-election to the Legislative Assemblies we had to fight with powerful opponents. I congratulate the Musalmans [Muslims] for having shown enormous grit and spirit throughout our trials. There was not a single by-election in which our opponents won against Muslim League candidates. In the last election to the U.P. Council, that is the Upper Chamber, the Muslim League's success was 100 percent. I do not want to weary you with details of what we have been able to do in the way of forging ahead in the direction of organizing the Muslim League. But I may tell you that it is going up by leaps and bounds. . . .

But a great deal yet remains to be done. I am sure from what I can see and hear that Muslim India is now conscious, is now awake, and the Muslim League has by now grown into such a strong institution that it cannot be destroyed by anybody, whoever he may happen to be. Men may come and men may go, but the League will live for ever. . . .

Now the question is, what is the best solution of this problem between the Hindus and the Musalmans? We have been considering—and a committee has been appointed to consider the various proposals. But whatever the final scheme for a constitution, I will present to you my views. . . .

The British Government and Parliament, and more so the British nation, have been, for many decades past, brought up and nurtured with settled notions about India's future; based on developments in their own country which have built up the British constitution, functioning now through the Houses of Parliament and the Cabinet system. Their concept of party-government, functioning on political planes, has become the ideal with them as the best form of government for every country; and the one-sided and powerful propaganda which naturally appeals to the British has led them into a serious blunder, in producing a constitution envisaged in the Government of India Act of 1935. We find that the leading statesmen of Great Britain, saturated with these notions, have in their pronouncements seriously asserted and expressed a hope that the passage of time will harmonize the inconsistent elements in India.

A leading journal like the London *Times*, commenting on the Government of India Act of 1935, wrote, "undoubtedly the difference between the Hindus and Muslims is not of religion in the strict sense of the word, but also of law and culture, that they may be said indeed to represent two entirely distinct and separate civilizations. However, in the course of time the superstitions will die out, and India will be moulded into a single nation." So, according to the London *Times*, the only difficulties are superstitions. These fundamental and deep-rooted differences, spiritual, economic, cultural, social and political, have been euphemized as mere 'superstitions'. But surely, it is a flagrant disregard of the past history of the subcontinent of India, as well as the fundamental Islamic conception of society, *vis-à-vis* that of Hinduism, to characterize them as mere 'superstitions'. Notwithstanding a thousand years of close contact, nationalities which are as divergent today as ever cannot at any time be expected to transform themselves into one nation merely by means of subjecting them to a democratic constitution and holding them forcibly together by unnatural and artificial methods of British Parliamentary Statutes. What the unitary Government of India for 150 years had failed to achieve cannot be realized by the imposition of a central federal government. It is inconceivable that the fiat or the writ of a government so constituted can ever command a willing and loyal obedience throughout the Subcontinent from various nationalities except by means of armed force behind it.

Autonomous National States

The problem in India is not of an inter-communal but manifestly of an international character, and it must be treated as such. So long as this basic and fundamental truth is not realized, any constitution that may be built will result in disaster and will prove destructive and harmful not only to the Musalmans, but also to the British and Hindus. If the British Government are really in earnest and sincere to secure the peace and happiness of the people of this Subcontinent, the only course open to us all is to allow the major nations separate homelands, by dividing India into 'autonomous national States'. There is no reason why these States should be antagonistic to each other. On the other hand, the rivalry and the natural desire and efforts on the part of the one (community) to dominate the social order and establish political supremacy over the other in the government of the country will disappear. It will lead more towards natural goodwill by international pacts between them (the states) and they can live in complete harmony with their neighbours. This will lead further to a friendly settlement all the more easily with regard to minorities by reciprocal arrangements and adjustments between the Muslim India and the Hindu India, which will far more adequately and effectively safeguard the rights and interests of Muslims and various other minorities.

It is extremely difficult to appreciate why our Hindu friends fail to understand the real nature of Islam and Hinduism. They are not religions in the strict sense of the word, but are, in fact, different and distinct social orders. It is a dream that the Hindus and Muslims can ever evolve a common nationality, and this misconception of one Indian nation has gone far beyond the limits, and is the cause of most of our troubles, and will lead India to destruction, if we fail to revise our notions in time. The Hindus and the Muslims belong to two different religious philosophies, social customs, and literature. They neither intermarry, nor interdine together, and indeed they belong to two different civilizations which are based mainly on conflicting ideas and conceptions. Their aspects on life and of life are different. It is quite clear that Hindus and Musalmans derive their inspiration from different sources of history. They have different epics, their heroes are different, and they have different episodes. Very often the hero of one is a foe of the other, and likewise, their victories and defeats overlap. To yoke together two such nations under a single State, one as a numerical minority and the other as a majority, must lead to growing discontent and the final destruction of any fabric that may be so built up for the government of such a State. . . .

Muslim India cannot accept any constitution which must necessarily result in a Hindu majority Government. Hindus and Muslims brought together under a democratic system forced upon the minorities can only mean Hindu Raj. Democracy of the kind with which the Congress High Command is enamoured would mean the complete destruction of what is most precious in Islam. We have had ample experience of the working of the provincial constitutions during the last two and a half years; and any repetition of such a Government must lead to civil war and raising private armies, as recommended by Mr. Gandhi to Hindus of Sukkur, when he said that they must defend themselves violently or non-violently, blow for blow; and if they could not, they must emigrate.

Musalmans are not a minority, as it is commonly known and understood. One has only got to look round. Even to-day, according to the British map of India, 4 out of 11 provinces, where the Muslims dominate more or less, are functioning notwithstanding the decision of the Hindu Congress High Command to non-co-operate and prepare for civil disobedience. Musalmans are a nation according to any definition of a nation, and they must have their homelands, their territory and their State. We wish to live in peace and harmony with our neighbours as a free and independent people. We wish our people to develop to the fullest our spiritual, cultural, economic, social and political life in a way that we think best, and in consonance with our own ideals and according to the genius of our people. Honesty demands—and the vital interests of millions of our people impose a sacred duty upon us to find—an honourable and peaceful solution which would be just and fair to all. But at the same time, we cannot be moved or diverted from our purpose and objective by threats or intimidations. We must be prepared to face all difficulties and consequences, make all the sacrifices that may be required of us to achieve the goal we have set in front of us. . . .

Conclusion

I have placed before you the task that lies ahead of us. Do you realize how big and stupendous it is? Do you realize that you cannot get freedom or independence by mere arguments? . . . I may tell you that unless you get this into your blood, unless you are prepared to take off your coats and are willing to sacrifice all that you can, and work selflessly, earnestly and sincerely for your people, you will never realize your aim. Friends, I therefore want you to make up your minds definitely, and then think of devices, and organize your people, strengthen your organization and consolidate the Musalmans all over India. I think that the masses are wide awake. They only want your guidance and lead. Come forward as servants of Islam, organize the people economically, socially, educationally and politically, and I am sure that you will be a power that will be accepted by everybody.

The Growth of Militant Islam in Pakistan

By Jessica Stern

*Beginning in the early 1970s, Pakistani political leaders supported and en-
couraged the growth of radical Islamic groups to advance their foreign policy goals in Kashmir and Afghanistan. The policy of supporting these groups
led to a concomitant rise in religious and sectarian violence, not only in Afghanistan and Kashmir but in Pakistan as well. Pakistan's military leader,
Pervez Musharraf, discontinued his support of many of these groups when he
joined the U.S.-led War on Terror in September 2001. However, analysts still
consider them to be a threat to peace and stability in Pakistan. In the following excerpt, written prior to Musharraf's change of policy, Jessica Stern, a
lecturer in public policy at Harvard University's John F. Kennedy School of
Government, reviews the growth of militant Islamic groups in Pakistan. According to Stern, one of the keys to reversing the growth of militant Islamic
groups is to improve the Pakistani education system and to strengthen Pakistan's democratic institutions.*

[In the spring of 2002] the U.S. State Department reported that
South Asia has replaced the Middle East as the leading locus of
terrorism in the world. Although much has been written about religious militants in the Middle East and Afghanistan, little is known
in the West about those in Pakistan—perhaps because they operate
mainly in Kashmir and, for now at least, do not threaten security outside South Asia. General Pervez Musharraf, Pakistan's military ruler,
calls them "freedom fighters" and admonishes the West not to con-
fuse jihad [holy war] with terrorism. Musharraf is right about the distinction—the jihad doctrine delineates acceptable war behavior and

Jessica Stern, "Pakistan's Jihad Culture," *Foreign Affairs*, vol. 79, November/December 2000,
pp. 115–26. Copyright © 2000 by the Council on Foreign Relations, Inc. Reproduced by permission.

explicitly outlaws terrorism—but he is wrong about the militant groups' activities. Both sides of the war in Kashmir—the Indian army and the Pakistani "mujahideen"—are targeting and killing thousands of civilians, violating both the Islamic "just war" tradition and international law.

Pakistan has two reasons to support the so-called mujahideen. First, the Pakistani military is determined to pay India back for allegedly fomenting separatism in what was once East Pakistan and in 1971 became Bangladesh. Second, India dwarfs Pakistan in population, economic strength, and military might. In 1998 India spent about two percent of its $469 billion gross domestic product [GDP] on defense, including an active armed force of more than 1.1 million personnel. In the same year, Pakistan spent about five percent of its $61 billion GDP on defense, yielding an active armed force only half the size of India's. The U.S. government estimates that India has 400,000 troops in Indian-held Kashmir—a force more than two-thirds as large as Pakistan's entire active army. The Pakistani government thus supports the irregulars as a relatively cheap way to keep Indian forces tied down.

What does such support entail? It includes, at a minimum, assisting the militants' passage into Indian-held Kashmir. This much Pakistani officials will admit, at least privately. The U.S. government believes that Pakistan also funds, trains, and equips the irregulars. Meanwhile, the Indian government claims that Pakistan uses them as an unofficial guerrilla force to carry out "dirty tricks," murders, and terrorism in India. Pakistan, in turn, accuses India's intelligence service of committing terrorism and killing hundreds of civilians in Pakistan.

Pakistan now faces a typical principal-agent problem: the interests of Pakistan (the principal) and those of the militant groups (the agent) are not fully aligned. Although the irregulars may serve Pakistan's interests in Kashmir when they target the Indian army, they also kill civilians and perform terrorism in violation of international norms and law. These crimes damage Pakistan's already fragile international reputation. Finally, and most important for Pakistanis, the militant groups that Pakistan supports and the Sunni sectarian killers that Pakistan claims it wants to wipe out overlap significantly. By facilitating the activities of the irregulars in Kashmir, the Pakistani government is inadvertently promoting internal sectarianism, supporting international terrorists, weakening the prospect for peace in Kashmir, damaging Pakistan's international image, spreading a narrow and violent version of Islam throughout the region, and increasing tensions with India—all against the interests of Pakistan as a whole.

Pakistan, Taliban-Style?

The war between India and Pakistan over the fate of Kashmir is as old as both states. When Pakistan was formally created in 1947, the rulers of Muslim-majority states that had existed within British India were given the option of joining India or Pakistan. The Hindu monarch of the predominantly Muslim state of Jammu and Kashmir chose India, prompted partly by a tribal rebellion in the state. Pakistan responded by sending in troops. The resultant fighting ended with a 1949 cease-fire, but the Pakistani government continued covertly to support volunteer guerrilla fighters in Kashmir. Islamabad argued then, as it does now, that it could not control the volunteers, who as individuals were not bound by the cease-fire agreement. . . .

Pakistani officials admit to having tried repeatedly to foment separatism in Kashmir in the decades following the 1949 cease-fire. These attempts were largely unsuccessful; when separatist violence broke out in the late 1980s, the movement was largely indigenous. For their part, Indian officials admit their own culpability in creating an intolerable situation in the region. They ignored Kashmir's significant economic troubles, rampant corruption, and rigged elections, and they intervened in Kashmiri politics in ways that contradicted India's own constitution. As American scholar Sumit Ganguly explains, the rigged 1987 state-assembly elections were the final straw in a series of insults, igniting, by 1989, widespread violent opposition. By 1992, Pakistani nationals and other graduates of the Afghan war [against the Soviet Union] were joining the fight in Kashmir.

What began as an indigenous, secular movement for independence has become an increasingly Islamist crusade to bring all of Kashmir under Pakistani control. Pakistan-based Islamist groups (along with Hizb-ul-Mujahideen, a Kashmir-based group created by Jamaat-e-Islami and partly funded by Pakistan) are now significantly more important than the secular Kashmir-based ones. The Indian government estimates that about 40 percent of the militants in Kashmir today are Pakistani or Afghan, and some 80 percent are teenagers. Although the exact size of the movement is unknown, the Indian government estimates that 3,000 to 4,000 "mujahideen" are in Kashmir at any given time.

Whatever their exact numbers, these Pakistani militant groups— among them, Lashkar-i-Taiba and Harkat-ul-Mujahideen—pose a long-term danger to international security, regional stability, and especially Pakistan itself. Although their current agenda is limited to "liberating" Kashmir, which they believe was annexed by India illegally, their next objective is to turn Pakistan into a truly Islamic state.

Islamabad supports these volunteers as a cheap way to keep India off balance. In the process, however, it is creating a monster that threatens to devour Pakistani society.

Schools of Hate

In Pakistan, as in many developing countries, education is not mandatory. The World Bank estimates that only 40 percent of Pakistanis are literate, and many rural areas lack public schools. Islamic religious schools—madrasahs—on the other hand, are located all over the country and provide not only free education, but also free food, housing, and clothing. In the poor areas of southern Punjab, madrasahs funded by the Sunni sectarian political party Sipah-e-Sahaba Pakistan (SSP) reportedly even pay parents for sending them their children.

In the 1980s, Pakistani dictator General Mohammad Zia-ul-Haq promoted the madrasahs as a way to garner the religious parties' support for his rule and to recruit troops for the anti-Soviet war in Afghanistan. At the time, many madrasahs were financed by the *zakat* (the Islamic tithe collected by the state), giving the government at least a modicum of control. But now, more and more religious schools are funded privately—by wealthy Pakistani industrialists at home or abroad, by private and government-funded nongovernmental organizations in the Persian Gulf states and Saudi Arabia, and by Iran. Without state supervision, these madrasahs are free to preach a narrow and violent version of Islam.

Most madrasahs offer only religious instruction, ignoring math, science, and other secular subjects important for functioning in modern society. As Maududi warned in his 1960 book, *First Principles of the Islamic State*, "those who choose the theological branch of learning generally keep themselves utterly ignorant of [secular subjects, thereby remaining] incapable of giving any lead to the people regarding modern political problems."

Even worse, some extremist madrasahs preach jihad without understanding the concept: They equate jihad—which most Islamic scholars interpret as the striving for justice (and principally an inner striving to purify the self)—with guerrilla warfare. These schools encourage their graduates, who often cannot find work because of their lack of practical education, to fulfill their "spiritual obligations" by fighting against Hindus in Kashmir or against Muslims of other sects in Pakistan. Pakistani officials estimate that 10 to 15 percent of the country's tens of thousands of madrasahs espouse such extremist ideologies.

Pakistan's interior minister Moinuddin Haider, for one, recognizes these problems. "The brand of Islam they are teaching is not good for Pakistan," he says. "Some, in the garb of religious training, are busy fanning sectarian violence, poisoning people's minds." In June 2002, Haider announced a reform plan that would require all madrasahs to register with the government, expand their curricula, disclose their financial resources, seek permission for admitting foreign students, and stop sending students to militant training camps.

This is not the first time the Pakistani government has announced such plans. And Haider's reforms so far seem to have failed, whether because of the regime's negligence or the madrasahs' refusal to be regulated, or both. Only about 4,350 of the estimated 40,000 to 50,000 madrasahs in Pakistan have registered with the government. Some are still sending students to training camps despite parents' instructions not to do so. Moreover, some chancellors are unwilling to expand their curricula, arguing that madrasahs are older than Pakistan itself—having been "designed 1,200 years ago in Iraq," according to the chancellor of the Khudamudeen madrasah. The chancellor of Darul Uloom Haqqania objects to what he calls the government's attempt to "destroy the spirit of the madrasahs under the cover of broadening their curriculum."

Mujibur Rehman Inqalabi, the SSP's second in command, told me that Haider's reform plan is "against Islam" and complains that where states have taken control of madrasahs, such as in Jordan and Egypt, "the engine of jihad is extinguished." America is right, he said: "Madrasahs are the supply line for jihad."

The Business of Jihad in Pakistan

If madrasahs supply the labor of "jihad," then wealthy Pakistanis and Arabs around the world supply the capital. On Eid-ul-Azha, the second most important Muslim holiday of the year, anyone who can afford to sacrifices an animal and gives the hide to charity. Pakistani militant groups solicit such hide donations, which they describe as a significant source of funding for their activities in Kashmir.

Most of the militant groups' funding, however, comes in the form of anonymous donations sent directly to their bank accounts. Lashkar-i-Taiba ("Army of the Pure"), a rapidly growing Ahle Hadith (Wahhabi) group, raises funds on the Internet. Lashkar and its parent organization, Markaz ad-Da'wa Wal Irshad (Center for Islamic Invitation and Guidance), have raised so much money, mostly from sympathetic Wahhabis in Saudi Arabia, that they are reportedly planning to open their own bank.

Individual "mujahideen" also benefit financially from this generous funding. They are in this for the loot, explains Ahmed Rashid, a prominent Pakistani journalist. One mid-level manager of Lashkar told me he earns 15,000 rupees a month—more than seven times what the average Pakistani makes, according to the World Bank. Top leaders of militant groups earn much more; one leader took me to see his mansion, which was staffed by servants and filled with expensive furniture. Operatives receive smaller salaries but win bonuses for successful missions. Such earnings are particularly attractive in a country with a 40 percent official poverty rate, according to Pakistani government statistics.

The United States and Saudi Arabia funneled some $3.5 billion into Afghanistan and Pakistan during the Afghan war, according to Milt Bearden, CIA station chief in Pakistan from 1986 to 1989. "Jihad," along with guns and drugs, became the most important business in the region. The business of "jihad"—what the late scholar Eqbal Ahmad dubbed "Jihad International, Inc."—continues to attract foreign investors, mostly wealthy Arabs in the Persian Gulf region and members of the Pakistani diaspora. (As World Bank economist Paul Collier observes, diaspora populations often prolong ethnic and religious conflicts by contributing not only capitol but also extremist rhetoric, since the fervor of the locals is undoubtedly held in check by the prospect of losing their own sons.)

As the so-called jihad movement continues to acquire its own financial momentum, it will become increasingly difficult for Pakistan to shut down, if and when it tries. As long as "Jihad International, Inc." is profitable, those with financial interests in the war will work to prolong it. And the longer the war in Kashmir lasts, the more entrenched these interests will become. . . .

Exporting Holy War

Pakistani militant groups are now exporting their version of jihad all over the world. The Khudamudeen madrasah, according to its chancellor, is training students from Burma, Nepal, Chechnya, Bangladesh, Afghanistan, Yemen, Mongolia, and Kuwait. Out of the 700 students at the madrasah, 127 are foreigners. Nearly half the student body at Darul Uloom Haqqania, the madrasah that created the Taliban, is from Afghanistan. It also trains students from Uzbekistan, Tajikistan, Russia, and Turkey, and is currently expanding its capacity to house foreign students from 100 to 500, its chancellor said. A Chechen student at the school told me his goal when he returned home was to fight Russians. And according to the U.S. State Department, Pakistani groups and individuals also help finance and train the Islamic Movement of Uzbekistan, a terrorist organization that aims to overthrow secular governments in Central Asia.

Many of the militant groups associated with radical madrasahs regularly proclaim their plans to bring "jihad" to India proper as well as to the West, which they believe is run by Jews. Lashkar-i-Taiba has announced its plans to "plant Islamic flags in Delhi, Tel Aviv, and Washington." One of Lashkar's Web sites includes a list of purported Jews working for the Clinton administration, including director of presidential personnel Robert Nash (an African American from Arkansas) and CIA director George Tenet (a Greek American). The group also accuses Israel of assisting India in Kashmir. Asked for a list of his favorite books, a leader of Harkat recommended the history of Hitler, who he said understood that "Jews and peace are incompatible." Several militant groups boast pictures of burning American flags on their calendars and posters. . . .

Pakistan's Road to Reform

Pakistan is a weak state, and government policies are making it weaker still. Its disastrous economy, exacerbated by a series of corrupt leaders, is at the root of many of its problems. Yet despite its poverty, Pakistan is spending hundreds of millions of dollars on weapons instead of schools and public health. Ironically, the government's "cost-saving" measures are even more troubling. In trying to save money in the short run by using irregulars in Kashmir and relying on madrasahs to educate its youth, Pakistan is pursuing a path that is likely to be disastrous in the long run, allowing a culture of violence to take root.

The United States has asked Pakistan to crack down on the militant groups and to close certain madrasahs, but America must do more than just scold. After all, the United States, along with Saudi Arabia, helped create the first international "jihad" to fight the Soviet Union during the Afghan war. "Does America expect us to send in the troops and shut the madrasahs down?" one official asks. "Jihad is a mindset. It developed over many years during the Afghan war. You can't change a mindset in 24 hours."

The most important contribution the United States can make, then, is to help strengthen Pakistan's secular education system. Because so much international aid to Pakistan has been diverted through corruption, both public and private assistance should come in the form of relatively nonfungible goods and services: books, buildings, teachers, and training, rather than money. Urdu-speaking teachers from around the world should be sent to Pakistan to help. And educational exchanges among students, scholars, journalists, and military officials should be encouraged and facilitated. Helping Pakistan educate its youth will not only cut off the culture of violence by reducing ignorance and poverty, it will also promote long-term economic development.

Moreover, assisting Pakistan will make the world a safer place. As observers frequently note, conflict between India and Pakistan over Kashmir is one of the most likely routes to nuclear war in the world today. The Pakistani militants' continued incursions into Indian-held Kashmir escalate the conflict, greatly increasing the risk of nuclear war between the two countries.

Although the United States can help, Pakistan must make its own changes. It must stamp out corruption, strengthen democratic institutions, and make education a much higher priority. But none of this can happen if Pakistan continues to devote an estimated 30 percent of its national budget to defense.

Most important, Pakistan must recognize the militant groups for what they are: dangerous gangs whose resources and reach continue to grow, threatening to destabilize the entire region. Pakistan's continued support of religious militant groups suggests that it does not recognize its own susceptibility to the culture of violence it has helped create. It should think again.

CHAPTER 2

The Kashmir Conflict with India and the Threat of Nuclear War

An Overview of the Kashmir Dispute Between India and Pakistan

By Victoria Schofield

Immediately after they gained independence from Britain in 1947, Pakistan and India went to war over the state of Kashmir, which continues to be the major source of conflict between the only two nuclear powers in South Asia. Victoria Schofield, a lecturer and historian who has traveled extensively in India and Pakistan, examines the history of the Kashmir dispute and offers a series of scenarios that might resolve it. Among these scenarios are a plebiscite allowing Kashmiris to determine their own fate and a formal agreement between India and Pakistan establishing the current Line of Control (LoC) in Kashmir as the legitimate border between India and Pakistan. Unfortunately, the obstacles to a resolution of the Kashmir dispute between India and Pakistan remain numerous.

It is nearly fifty years since the conflict over the former princely state of Jammu and Kashmir[1] began. Regrettably, there are many troublespots in the world all needing attention, but surely Kashmir must rank as one of the most important? The dispute arose out of exceptional circumstances: Karan Singh, son of the last Maharaja of Jammu and Kashmir, spoke of the whole process of independence and partition as being a "once in a millennium historical phenomenon", and the Kashmir issue today clearly has its origins in 1947. Al-

1. "Jammu and Kashmir" is the name for the Indian-controlled portion of Kashmir.

Victoria Schofield, "Kashmir—Today, Tomorrow?" *Asian Affairs*, vol. 28, October 1997, pp. 315–24. Copyright © 1997 by American-Asian Educational Exchange, Inc. Reproduced by permission.

though the Indian Government does not like calling the Kashmir issue the "unfinished business of partition", there remain many people in Pakistan and within the state of Jammu and Kashmir who believe that the issue has never been fully resolved. At the same time, it is hard to continue to generate interest in a problem which seems to have no solution and, from a Western perspective, is remote. People talk of donor fatigue for worthy causes which are like bottomless pits—there is also the tendency for people to prefer to turn their backs on issues that appear insoluble.

Kashmir does, however, deserve attention not just because it is a beautiful place, not just because—as American foreign policy experts have assessed—it may constitute one of the most likely flashpoints for conflict in the region, possibly involving nuclear weapons, but because people are suffering and dying, families have been separated, sons have been killed, women have been raped, innocent people killed in the crossfire. All too often when we talk about Kashmir or any place where civil war is being waged, we tend to talk in broad terms about governments and countries without paying enough attention to the people on the ground who are the most affected by the continuing strife, wherever their loyalties lie. . . .

It is self-evident that the relationship between India and Pakistan could have been quite different had the issue over the future of Jammu and Kashmir not been left hanging. Cynics may argue that had India and Pakistan not had Kashmir to argue about, they would have found something else. But I prefer to tread along the path of optimism and consider that the governments of both Pakistan and India would like to see a way to resolve their political differences, if only they could do so without losing face. I also believe that the international community would prefer to see genuine peace in the valley of Kashmir and more amicable relations between India and Pakistan.

The History of the Kashmir Dispute

The factual history of the Kashmir dispute is well known: how the leaders of the new Pakistan expected to have the state of Jammu and Kashmir included within its borders in 1947, because the majority of its population was Muslim. Although the princes of the 565 princely states did not fall under the direction of the partition council, they had all been given a clear directive by the Viceroy, Lord Mountbatten, that, when deciding their future allegiance, they should take into account their geographical position and the composition of their people. The problem with the state of Jammu and Kashmir was that geographically it could be reached through either India or Pakistan. And the Maharaja—Hari Singh—who was a Hindu, evidently did not want to join

Pakistan, which would have put a considerable number of Hindus in the minority as well as the Buddhists in Ladakh [an area in northern Kashmir]. As his son relates in his autobiography, "when the crucial moment came" his father was alone and friendless, and consequently did nothing. Only when there was unrest in Poonch and large numbers of Pathan tribesmen from the North-West Frontier invaded his state did he request assistance from India. It is interesting that at this juncture Mountbatten, who, after independence in August 1947 became Governor-General of India, was instrumental in persuading the Maharaja to accede to India before giving assistance, because otherwise he feared that there would be an inter-dominion war. Mountbatten has since been criticised for this action; had the accession not taken place, it might have been easier to hold a referendum or plebiscite. As Mountbatten's biographer Philip Ziegler writes:

> If there had been no accession, the Indian presence in Kashmir would have been more evidently temporary, the possibility of a properly constituted referendum have become more real. By exaggerated legalism the Governor-General helped bring about the result he most feared: the protracted occupation of Kashmir by India with no attempt to show that it enjoyed popular support.

Although the Indian government maintains that the action was supported by Sheikh [Muhammad] Abdullah, Kashmir's popular leader, to this day the Pakistanis assert that the Maharaja took the decision under duress and that he had no mandate to accede to India on behalf of his people because he had fled from the capital of his state, Srinagar, to the comparative safety of Jammu.

Conflicting Demands

The problems confronting a resolution of the Kashmir issue today still arise primarily from the character of the state and its strategic position high up in the Himalayas, close to China and the former Soviet Union. Had the state been an obvious homogeneous unit it would have been much easier to decide its future. But, although the recent troubles have taken place primarily in the valley, as protagonists for a change to the status quo continually point out, the future of the entire state is involved—an area covering over 80,000 square miles, with a wide range of language, religion and culture. The obvious divisions within the state make a solution even harder to reach; what one section of the population might agree to, another will not. The people of the predominantly Buddhist, sparsely populated area of Ladakh have consistently and recently even more vociferously rejected political domination by the politicians of the valley, and it seems more than likely that they would prefer to work out some autonomous relationship with the Government of India rather than throw their lot in with the demands of the Kashmiri Muslims of the valley. The predominantly Hindu areas of Jammu have always had difficulty in reconciling themselves to the shift in emphasis from Jammu to Srinagar which occurred after independence. Balraj Puri, the well-known Jammu commentator, was entirely accurate when he wrote:

> Jammu and Kashmir which were united in 1846 are not known to have been mutually well adjusted regions of the state they comprise. The political and administrative set up after 1947 was as conducive to regional tensions as the one it had replaced.

As the Indian government has often pointed out, the valley's numerical superiority has given it the loudest voice. But, even so, it is impossible to talk of unity there. Farooq Abdullah, leader of the National Conference and Chief Minister, is as much a Kashmiri Muslim as Omar Farooq, who heads the All Parties *Hurriyat*—or Freedom—Conference, yet they currently have radically different viewpoints on the future of the state. The Kashmiri Pandits must also be given a say in their future. Then there are the Gujar Muslims, whose objectives may differ from those of the Kashmiri-speaking valley Muslims, as may those of the Muslims of the Kargil area in Ladakh. . . .

The Plebiscite Option in Kashmir

In any change to the status quo, the first issue which must be faced is that of the plebiscite—which still has tremendous appeal as a method for ascertaining the wishes of the people. However much the Indian government maintains that the UN resolutions of 1948 and 1949 [establishing a cease-fire in hostilities between India and Pakistan] are no longer relevant, it is impossible to engage any Kashmiri in a political conversation in the valley without reverting to talking about the issue of plebiscite. "We were promised a plebiscite—we are still waiting for it" is the usual comment from taxi drivers and shopkeepers in the valley. The issue was one which Sir Owen Dixon, on behalf of the UN, worked very hard to resolve in 1950.

But the plebiscite itself raises several questions: Would it be possible, in today's world, to hold a plebiscite as envisaged by the UN resolutions and under what conditions? Would the outcome of a plebiscite—again in today's world—be a fair way of determining the state's future? Should a plebiscite be held on a unitary basis throughout the entire state (as stipulated by the UN resolutions and preferred by Pakistan) or would it in fact be better, as Owen Dixon had suggested, to permit the people of the various regions to vote? Although this idea and variations—for example, a plebiscite only in the valley—have been rejected, might they not now be reconsidered? In view of the general attachment to the idea of holding a plebiscite, should it not at least remain on the drawing board for future discussion, in which case, should serious consideration be given to making it a regional plebiscite, which might be a fairer way of giving all parties a say in their future? The circumstances for holding a plebiscite, including demilitarisation, would once more have to be agreed upon so that the people did not feel intimidated while exercising their right to vote. Perhaps, in this regard, the UN might be more effective in assuaging the fears of both India and Pakistan, regarding their security concerns, than it was in the late 1940s and early 1950s.

The next problem is what could be on the agenda of the plebiscite? In the UN resolutions, the choice was given to accession between India and Pakistan. But now there is the inescapable proposal of the third option [independence]—rejected by Pakistan, but very clearly an objective in the minds of many of the Kashmiris, who see it as enshrined in the 1948 UN resolution, which does not stipulate a choice between India or Pakistan but merely says that the future of the state should be decided according to the will of the people. How therefore to include the third option? One of the problems about the resolutions is that they are often considered to have been mandatory. But they are not legally binding—they are only recommendations. If we accept this, then might some amendments be possible? Or should the discontented Kashmiris give up the idea of a third option being included because neither Pakistan nor India would tolerate the possibility of an independent state between them?

The India Element

There is, of course, a far greater hurdle to cross. How to persuade India to discuss any proposals regarding the valley of Kashmir which might result in a loss of land that it considers to be an integral part of the Union. All along, this has been the reason why there has been no meaningful dialogue, and it will be interesting to see how future discussions differ from earlier initiatives. The Indo-Pakistani talks of 1962–3 represent the last time India was prepared to submit to third-party mediators, when the Anglo-American team of Sir Duncan Sandys and Averill Harriman visited Islamabad and Delhi. Their reason for doing so was mainly because the Indian government was feeling particularly vulnerable after its 1962 defeat by China in the border war. For the future, then, what would make the Indian government prepared firstly, to negotiate and secondly, to make any concessions? These questions have to be faced before any solution is possible. I have attended many debates and seminars where a wide range of optimistic suggestions are made, but commentators seem to overlook the fact that there has to be a pressing reason for the Government of India to want to submit to them.

The idea of improved relations is obviously appealing for the people who would like to visit each other and their relatives more freely, but what is the real incentive for the governments? Trade and education exchanges are often suggested as being a conductive carrot to a thaw in relations, but, from the Indian perspective, that does not mean making any concessions over Kashmir. Reducing India's military commitments and budget is an obvious incentive for flexibility. But to date, with between 300,000 to 800,000 Indian soldiers in Kashmir, they have managed to sustain their presence without any obvious pressing need for withdrawal.

It has also been suggested that India might want a permanent seat on the UN Security Council in return for a settlement over Kashmir. That is one possibility, although it is unlikely that India would submit to such an obvious bribe. There are also the rather fantastic suggestions of economic sanctions and/or war waged by Britain and/or the United States against India in order to make the government comply with the UN resolutions. These suggestions have generally emanated from Pakistani commentators, whose emotion and sense of injustice has often blinded them to the impracticalities of such a venture. Neither Britain nor the United States is prepared to jeopardise its relationship with India because of Kashmir, which is why it will be interesting to see how [British] Prime Minister [Tony] Blair actually puts into practice the Labour Party's commitment to the Kashmir issue. Condemning human rights abuses in the valley is one thing, but pressurising India to give up territory which it believes is part of the Union is quite different. . . .

Future Scenarios for the Kashmir Conflict

For the future, four possible scenarios emerge. The first is the maintenance of the status quo by which neither Pakistan nor India loses anything it has already got, but which leaves Pakistan still mentally preoccupied with its claim on Kashmir, as well as militancy and frustration amongst the Kashmiris. In an age of readily available lethal weapons it is too simplistic to hope that those who have not had their ambitions fulfilled will simply lay down their guns and pick up their cricket bats. India has hoped for a Punjab solution, but so far it has not materialised. Kashmir is not the Punjab; the Punjab was never promised that the future of the people could be decided by a free, fair and impartial plebiscite according to recommendations passed by the UN Security Council. The issues are too emotive, too powerful to forget. If one generation is silenced, the next will read about the plebiscite and take up arms again.

The second scenario involves a total change of heart on the part of the Pakistanis, which is obviously what the Indian government is hoping for: that, beset by its own economic problems, the Government of Pakistan realises that it cannot continue to sustain its military budget any more and that, with an instant stroke of the pen, actually agrees to the maintenance of the status quo by recognising that the line of control is the international frontier. This would rid Pakistan of its continual preoccupation with the Kashmiris, who have shown no whole-hearted desire to join Pakistan in the 1990s and who could ultimately prove as much of a problem to Pakistan as they have to India. But, with Gohar Ayub, Sharif's foreign secretary, stating that Pakistan's position on Kashmir is immutable, the prognosis for such a scenario is most unlikely, however real it may have appeared in the minds of the Indians after [the 1971 war with Pakistan]. Recognising the line of control as an international border is also not as easy as it sounds, because it leaves India exposed at a number of points along the border, most notably at the Haji Pir pass which is held by Pakistan. If the Indians request a straightening of the line to safeguard their border, this would in turn leave Pakistan militarily exposed.

The third and official optimum Pakistani scenario is for the UN resolutions to be observed, which they seem somehow to hope would result in a majority vote for Kashmir to join Pakistan. The drawback to this scenario is firstly, that it is not supported by India, secondly, it does not have the support of many of the Kashmiris because the UN resolutions do not include the third option [of independence].

The fourth and last scenario involves a leap of faith on behalf of India and Pakistan and requires them both to have a degree of political maturity which their fifty years of independence has given them, to look into the future and ask themselves if they still want to be haggling over Kashmir in another fifty years' time or if they could both give a little; if both countries could agree to wanting to live peacefully and wanting to see the Kashmiris do likewise, the fourth scenario would be to return to the drawing board—perhaps designed as a round table—with as many delegates from its component parts as are needed to give vent to the varying viewpoints. This might be made easier through the auspices of an international mediator, but if it can be achieved through bilateral discussions, including representation from the Kashmiris, then so much the better. As the Indian writer Pran Chopra says, it would be far better if Pakistan and India could resolve their differences themselves "rather than being summoned to appear at alien tables by third countries".

Key items on the agenda would be how best to lay to rest the issue of the plebiscite, by holding some form of referendum or plebiscite, demilitarisation of the valley with assistance from the United Nations, the possibility of a soft border between Azad Kashmir [Pakistani-controlled Kashmir] and the valley, security provisions for Ladakh and the Northern Areas, as well as aid to restore the valley's shattered economy. Despite past intransigence, radical changes can take place; frontiers can be re-drawn—or softened. One only has to look at the extraordinary demise of the Soviet Union, which ten or fifteen years ago, one might have thought impossible; or the reunification of the two parts of Germany, or, most recently, the unexpected political changes in South Africa.

In conclusion, I would like to record a conversation which I had with an Indian civil servant who was sympathetic to the emotional wishes of the Kashmiris, if not to their geographical ambitions. "Independence," he said, "you come and ask me if Kashmiris want independence. But you should use their term *azadi—azadi* means freedom; what the Kashmiris want is freedom to lead their own lives and to be themselves with dignity and respect, wherever they can get it". So whether it is called 'autonomy' or 'independence', the important issue today is to determine how the Kashmiris can lead their own lives, without domination from either India or Pakistan. Could this objective not be reached, bearing in mind the issues I have discussed on the agenda, without a loss of face for India or Pakistan? As Sheikh Abdullah said when he visited Pakistan in 1964, no one must be left with a sense of defeat. Whatever animosity may have existed between the protagonists, they will always be neighbours. Without the consent of both India and Pakistan, there can be no change to the status quo—and no *azadi*.

Pakistan's Position on Nuclear Proliferation in South Asia

By Riaz Mohammad Khan

Riaz Mohammad Khan is currently a spokesman for the Pakistani Ministry of Foreign Affairs and was recently the Pakistan ambassador to Belgium, Luxembourg, and the European Union. In the following selection, Khan argues that Pakistan had no choice but to respond to India's nuclear tests in May 1998 with tests of its own. Khan claims that the Pakistani tests neutralized India's military advantage over Pakistan by creating a credible deterrent against Indian military adventurism in the region, especially in Kashmir. Despite heavy international criticism, Khan maintains that Pakistan needed to develop a nuclear weapons program to maintain its security and pursue its foreign policy goals.

I will try to recapitulate briefly Pakistan's positions and concerns relating to nuclear issues. Our concerns go back to 1968 when the Nuclear Non-Proliferation Treaty (NPT) was being negotiated and Pakistan was one of the few countries who, at that time, tried to work for positive assurances for non-nuclear weapons states. In 1974, when India exploded its first nuclear device, Pakistan's position assumed a strong regional perspective, rooted in our very well-known security concerns. Since then, we have taken a number of initiatives aimed bilaterally at India and also in a regional context, such as agreeing on a nuclear test ban or signing the NPT together with India. The last such initiative was taken in 1992 when Prime Minister

Riaz Mohammad Khan, "South Asia Goes Nuclear: Indian and Pakistani Positions," *Contemporary South Asia*, vol. 7, 1998, pp. 193–200. Copyright © 1998 by Riaz Mohammad Khan. Reproduced by permission.

Nawaz Sharif suggested that Pakistan and India, along with China, the USA and Russia, should work out an agreement which could serve the objective of nuclear non-proliferation in the region.

Recently, Pakistan became concerned by some of the statements which were coming out during the Indian general election campaign. We knew that the Bharatiya Janata Party (BJP) election programme included conducting nuclear tests and increasing military spending. So we were worried, and in February/March 1998 our prime minister wrote to a number of heads of government informing them that if India conducted nuclear tests it would bring enormous pressure upon Pakistan, and Pakistan would be constrained to follow suit. He urged the international community and Western governments to do something to dissuade India from taking such a step. I think it was in April that [US] Ambassador Bill Richardson and [US Deputy Secretary of State] Strobe Talbot visited New Delhi and Islamabad. At that time we were told that the Indian government had no intention to carry out nuclear tests.

In May 1998, when India conducted its nuclear tests, the first step we took was to send envoys to Beijing and to Washington in an attempt to explore the possibility of so-called 'positive assurances'. As we had expected, the response was that such assurances were not possible. We were also very concerned about statements made by Indian leaders and officials saying that Pakistan must now realise that the strategic balance had changed, and that Pakistan would be dealt with firmly. This generated a great deal of public pressure upon the government and there was no other option but to conduct our own nuclear tests. Pakistan had to respond to establish a deterrence defence. In the absence of deterrence, there was a real danger of military adventurism against Pakistan.

Security Concerns

Our current position is that we surely do not want a nuclear arms race. We have declared a unilateral moratorium on further nuclear tests. At present, we have also reiterated one of the assurances which we had given earlier; namely, that we will not pass on this nuclear technology to any other country. This has been reaffirmed following the nuclear tests. There have been a number of resolutions and talk about asking Pakistan and India to ratify the Comprehensive Test Ban Treaty (CTBT) and the NPT, or participate in negotiations for controls of nuclear materials. Pakistan is seriously examining these issues, but as far as the NPT is concerned, given that there is now a qualitatively different situation in South Asia, it would be quite unrealistic to talk about a nuclear non-proliferation regime for South

Asia. Perhaps it is not just for Pakistan and India to consider how they should adhere to the NPT, but it is also for the other signatories of the treaty to consider how they could bring these two countries within the regime of the NPT.

I spoke earlier about Pakistan's regional perspective and our security concerns. Kashmir has been the core issue, the source of all our security concerns in the region, and we desire meaningful dialogue with India on this issue. We hope that the meeting between the two prime ministers in July 1998 [at the South Asian Association for Regional Cooperation (SAARC) meeting in Colombo] will lead to some constructive positive results. We also appreciate the initiatives taken by other countries to help to resolve the conflict. We are very grateful for these initiatives, because we feel that international concern can help the two countries to make progress towards the resolution of these conflicts, as well as strengthening confidence-building measures.

We agree with India on one issue: that any attempt by the international community to punish Pakistan and India will not help to resolve any problem. Pakistan, of course, has experienced sanctions in the past, and we were under sanctions from 1977–1981 precisely because of the nuclear issue. However, instead of sanctions, there is a need for exploring what can be done to address the security concerns in the region. . . .

Pakistan's Need for a Nuclear Deterrent

There were questions concerning how people perceived international reaction to these tests. I am sure that perceptions would be different in Pakistan and India because our people look at our tests as a necessary response, because we thought it would have been extremely dangerous for our security had we not established a deterrence. Our purpose was to establish deterrence. Pakistanis feel that the world should understand the pressure to which they were subjected following the Indian tests. . . .

Of course, harsh reactions have come mainly from the West, not from elsewhere. Some people in the West see India and Pakistan as behaving irresponsibly with this technology. I am sure that this argument is untenable. The countries which had developed this capability earlier also saw other countries [conducting nuclear tests] as 'irresponsible' at a particular point of time. For example, China after 1964 and until the 1970s was not regarded as very responsible by some of the Western countries, nor was the Soviet Union in the 1950s. The question of responsibility and morality is not relevant. But the argument of deterrence, which had been applicable in Europe, is.

I certainly do not want to say that everything is quiet and calm in South Asia; we do have problems and, as I mentioned earlier, our whole perception of the nuclear issue has been rooted in the regional context and in our security concerns, the main issue being Kashmir. If problems remain, they have consequences, and sometimes their consequences can be more intolerable for some people than the problem itself. For some of the Western countries, this is precisely what happened. The continuation of the [Kashmir] problem has led to this current situation. But we would like, as we have tried in the past, to resolve our problems with India. We desire—and I am sure that the Indian leadership would also want—our resources to be devoted to the well-being of our people. But again, you have to look at things in a historical context. Europe is making this argument [for non-proliferation in South Asia] because they are in a different phase of history. After all, they have also seen a lot in their recent history. We probably would not go to that extent in our region, but there are problems and perceptions that create responses and reactions. There is the reality that Pakistan has to maintain a strong defence. If this [Kashmir] problem had not been there, Pakistan would have not taken this course.

The nuclear course was certainly not something that we had chosen for ourselves. You might recall that in 1967, France had offered us a nuclear reprocessing plant and at that time we had refused, saying we did not need it. It was after 1974 [India's first nuclear test] when a new situation arose, that we therefore had to respond. We responded in two ways; one was the regional approach for nuclear non-proliferation, the other was to have our own programme.

Someone asked a question about why there was no focus to our [nuclear] programme. Certainly there was a great deal of focus to our programme, and that is why we were put under sanctions from 1977–1981. They were lifted for very obvious reasons [the Soviet intervention in Afghanistan], but in 1990, as soon as the Soviet troops withdrew from Afghanistan, the sanctions were reinstated. They have remained until today. There was discrimination against Pakistan on the nuclear issue. We have suffered. . . .

Nonetheless, countries simply cannot sit and wait, they have to devise new strategies. Therefore, we have to address the situation which we did by developing our missile programme.

The Social Costs of Nuclear Proliferation

By Mohammed Ahmedullah

Mohammed Ahmedullah is the online editor of Military Technology, *a strategic affairs writer in New Delhi, India, and was recently a visiting fellow for the* Bulletin of the Atomic Scientists. *In the article below, Ahmedullah describes the numerous social costs associated with the conflict between Pakistan and India, especially the increase in poverty over the last decade. In making his case, the author points out the large amount of money that both governments spend on their nuclear programs—money that could be used to alleviate poverty and to improve the infrastructure of two of the most densely populated countries in the world. Not only have the nuclear programs harmed social progress, Ahmedullah contends, but the conflict between India and Pakistan has inhibited the development of a mutually beneficial trading relationship between the two countries that could promote lasting peace in the region.*

A n Indian television commercial for a local whiskey shows two stern-faced border guards, one in the khaki of the Pakistani army, the other in Indian army olive green. They stare intently at one another. Then the guard in olive green pulls out a bottle of whiskey and offers it to the other. After a little hesitation, the guard in khaki reaches for the bottle from behind a barbed wire fence and takes a swig.

Fast forward to reality. Visitors to the Wagah border post in Punjab are struck by the unusual bonhomie among soldiers from both sides. When Indian and Pakistani patrols run into one another, they shake hands, crack jokes, and inquire about each other's families. It is common knowledge that Indian liquor may change hands during these encounters. And this has been going on since 1947, unaffected by wars, terrorists, missiles tests, or nuclear blasts.

India and Pakistan, South Asia's quarrelsome neighbors, may be pointing nukes at one another, but theirs is a love-hate relationship. Just months after New Delhi and Islamabad tested nuclear weapons in May 1998, and while they were in the midst of testing missile delivery systems, Indian Prime Minister Atal Behari Vajpayee rode a bus to Lahore to shake hands on a trade pact with his Pakistani counterpart, Nawaz Sharif. Vajpayee composed a poem on not fighting wars, which Sharif read aloud for the occasion.

Barely four months later, Pakistan began the Kargil intrusion, its most organized military action against India since the 1971 war. Still, the Kargil war did not stop the regularly scheduled bus that leaves New Delhi for Lahore. The bus is a microcosm of potential cross-border trade—enterprising passengers carry small amounts of goods in demand on the other side—medicines, textiles, and tea bound for Pakistan, dried fruit and cosmetics headed for India.

The official trade between the two countries is less than a tenth of its potential. But Pakistan's black market sells a variety of Indian goods—tea, liquor, textiles, pharmaceuticals, automobile tires, processed food, and other items—that are either smuggled in or imported indirectly via a third country. Pakistan also depends largely on India for its supply of cheap hard liquor.

India and Pakistan simply cannot come to terms with the fact that there is money to be made from one another. Every time an initiative designed to further trade ties is undertaken, it is pushed back by war, terrorism, or fundamentalist lobbying.

Less than Rosy

It has been more than two years since India and Pakistan exploded underground nuclear devices and declared themselves nuclear powers. Both believed that flexing their nuclear muscles would give them an impenetrable security cover, reducing their need for conventional military hardware and permitting a greater concentration of resources on economic development. It was as if nukes were an internal cleansing mechanism that would rid the two impoverished countries of all the problems they faced.

But events of the past two years have turned that rosy belief topsy-turvy. If anything, Pakistan and India are less secure. Their currencies are weaker and economic growth has declined, unemployment increased, and investment stagnated.

The undeclared war in Kashmir in May 1999 further worsened the relationship between the two neighbors, worrying the international community that the two might blunder into the use of nuclear weapons.

The war cost India $2 million a day for two months, and the bill for Pakistan could not have been less. In the immediate few months after the war, inflation had shot up by 20 percent in India, and in Pakistan prices of essential commodities had almost doubled. However, bumper crops in 1999–2000 all over the subcontinent, where the primary economic activity is agriculture, saved the two countries from economic disaster.

Some economic recovery has been made by both India and Pakistan since Kargil. A stable government in India and Gen. Pervez Musharraf's attempts to cleanse corruption in Pakistan have helped both countries pull back from the brink.

Pakistan, more than India, has a long way to go before its public treasury can begin to earn the admiration of the World Bank and the International Monetary Fund (IMF). Pakistan has been unable to secure release of a $280 million loan, part of a $1.6 billion IMF credit that was negotiated in 1997. The IMF ruled that since Pakistan had not improved its economy since the last loan, the next installment would be delayed pending structural adjustments. Pakistan has also sought to reschedule a $600 million Eurobond loan and an $877 million debt to foreign banks, which gives one a fair idea of the state of its economy.

India's economy may be better managed than Pakistan's, but it is a long way from reaching the pre-1998 level of foreign investment. Despite Bill Clinton's visit in March 2000, New Delhi has been unable to interest American, European, or Japanese investors in its industrial sectors. Foreign investment in fiscal 1999–2000 was $8.3 billion, compared to $9.6 billion in 1997–98. The only silver lining has been the increase in software exports, but most software is created on contract to foreign firms.

The bad blood created by the May 1998 nuclear tests continues to frighten foreign investors, and foreign aid to social sectors is at a low point. Although the bumper harvest has meant there is no food shortage for India's 1 billion people, getting money to make improvements in electricity, telecommunications, water, and roads continues to be a major problem. Little effort has gone into lifting the country's 400 million poor out of abject poverty. . . .

Pakistan's Costs

Pakistan's eat-grass-but-build-nuclear-weapons attitude has cost it dearly. While it was long believed in India that the aid China gave to the Pakistani nuclear weapons program was a gratis effort to counter India, it has turned out that Pakistan paid the Chinese for their help. That admission was made in 1998 by Pakistan's nuclear weapons program chief, Abdul Qadir Khan. The 1986 Sino-Pakistan agreement on atomic energy is believed to have been a commercial deal designed to formalize what until then had been a clandestine transaction. In return, Pakistan is reported to have received a single warhead design and sufficient highly enriched uranium to build a few weapons. The design of the 25-kiloton device Pakistan exploded in 1999 is said to be the same as the one used in China's fourth nuclear test, which was an atmospheric test using a ballistic missile launch. It was widely reported in the mid-1990s that Pakistan's stockpile consisted of as many as 10 nuclear warheads based on a Chinese design.

Although the United States supported Pakistan in an effort to rid Afghanistan of its Soviet occupation, it was suspicious about Pakistan's nuclear ambitions. As long as Pakistan remained vital to U.S. interests in Afghanistan, however, no action was taken to cut off support. Once the Soviets pulled out, the United States ended military assistance to Pakistan and severely curtailed economic aid.

Pakistan's thirst for nuclear weapons deprived it of conventional weapons aid as well. If Pakistan had not procured Chinese nuclear weapons and North Korean missiles, it could have received a great deal of sophisticated American weaponry, mostly in the form of aid. And if Pakistan had heeded international appeals to refrain from testing after the May 1998 Indian tests, it would have moved into the same league as Israel and Egypt as far as U.S. weapons largesse was concerned. A golden opportunity was squandered.

The real cost of Pakistan's nuclear program is far higher than the estimated $5 billion would indicate. The loss of U.S. military and economic support cost several times as much. And the burden caused by the end of aid from other Western countries and the rejection of Pakistani goods in many Western markets as punishment for developing nuclear weapons has added to the cost.

Pakistan then followed up on the tests with a series of economically disastrous measures. The day after the tests in May 1998, Pakistan froze all of its citizens' foreign currency accounts to prevent capital flight. Although it lifted the freeze the next day, the damage was done; Pakistani banks suffered a run on their foreign currency accounts. Pakistan's main hard currency source, its nationals who work in the oil-rich Gulf, cut their repatriation rate, hoping to gain more from the rapidly slipping rupee. Within a month, the Pakistani rupee had lost 25 percent of its value.

Pakistan was already subject to some U.S. sanctions, imposed in

1990 under the Pressler amendment—$650 million in military and humanitarian aid was cut off when the president was unable to certify that Pakistan did not possess a nuclear device. After Pakistan's tests, President Clinton was required by law (including the Glenn amendment, a part of the Arms Export Control Act) to impose further sanctions.

With $37 billion in foreign debt (more than half of the country's total gross domestic product), a monthly trade deficit of $150 million, foreign exchange reserves of only $1.3 billion, and interest payments of $200–500 million due each month, Pakistan is an economic mess. . . .

India's Costs

The cost to India jumped skyward after its nuclear tests, as it became clear that India wanted a credible nuclear deterrent with an effective delivery system. The cost for the deterrent has been variously estimated at $10–25 billion over the next 10 years.

The nuclear weapons program and the social burden it imposes has been sharply criticized at home. S.R. Valluri, a well-known aerospace scientist and opponent of India's nuclear weaponization policy, has given vent to what a lot of people think in India: "The cost of a meaningful nuclear deterrent and its delivery systems, taking a requirement of 150 warheads, works out to about $70 billion. The Human Resources Development Ministry had to drop a plan to provide basic education to all school-age children as it demanded an investment of a like amount over 15 years."

In fact, many intellectuals within India blame the government for initiating the nuclear arms race with Pakistan. "In three wars with Pakistan, we did not need nuclear arms to defeat them. Pakistan's nuclear weapons program was in response to India's 1974 testing," says Valluri. "If the Indian nuclear weapons program is not aimed at Pakistan but at China, as some Indian politicians would like us to believe, then 150 warheads is insufficient. China has over 300 of them, including long-range missiles to deliver them. Does this mean India should match China bomb for bomb and missile for missile, irrespective of the cost?"

Interestingly, India's nuclear weapons program is not funded out of the defense budget, but by its Department of Atomic Energy (DAE). The DAE's budget (presumably for nuclear power programs and research) increased by 25 percent [between 1998 and 2000].

In any case, the cost of the nuclear deterrent is a lot less for India than it is for Pakistan. That is because both India's nuclear weapons and its missile programs are indigenous, requiring no outgo of hard currency. It might make more economic sense for India to have a nuclear deterrent with conventional ballistic and cruise missiles as offensive weapons than it would be to have a more extensive conventional arms capability, which it pays for in hard currency. In [recent] years, India has pumped money into the Russian economy with several high-profile purchases worth more than $3 billion.

What They Could Gain from Each Other

If India and Pakistan took the Lahore declaration seriously and pursued cross-border trade, they could gain a lot from one another.

History has shown that both countries have grown during periods of relative calm between wars and when there was no terrorism. In the years between wars—1967–1970 and 1975–1980—key economic indicators like job creation, health care, education, and agriculture all showed growth.

Although both economies are generally stagnant, there was one period of rapid growth. From 1992 to 1996, Indian Prime Minister P.V. Narasimha Rao initiated an economic reform program. The period was marked by a steep drop in military expenditures as Rao delayed major weapons acquisitions and turned down requests from India's defense scientists to conduct nuclear tests. Pakistan, too, began attracting foreign investment and took fewer potshots at India. Both economies grew at their most impressive levels since independence.

The Indian economy's growth rate crossed the 7 percent mark and Pakistan's was around 6.5—one percentage point higher than that achieved in the late 1960s and late 1970s, the other periods marked by less war hysteria and more focus on development.

In 1992 and 1993, Indian industry, which had been eyeing the 130 million Pakistanis as a ready market for its goods (Indian consumer goods brands are well-known in Pakistan), sent business delegations to Lahore and Islamabad. Deals to export Indian products were agreed to and official cross-border trade reached $250 million in 1995, a record. For the first time, the Indian Industry Association welcomed a trade delegation from Pakistan.

This was also a period of rapid growth in Southeast Asia, and the possibility of conflict between the two countries was put firmly on the back burner. Following India's lead in opening its economy, Pakistan also invited foreign investment.

Most economists agree that since the nuclear tests in May 1998, the Indian economy has declined. The rate of growth in 1998–99 and 1999–2000 averaged 5.5 percent, down from the anticipated rate of

6.5 percent. The Indian government admits that economic sanctions and the fall in investor confidence were largely to blame. . . .

Nuclearization and Poverty

Nuclear bombs notwithstanding, another bomb gets bigger by the day—the population bomb. India's 1 billion and Pakistan's 130 million make their countries among the most densely populated in the world.

On May 11, 2000, India celebrated the second anniversary of the 1998 nuclear blasts . . . officially declared "Technology Day." At about the same time, the Indian population crossed the 1 billion mark. Indian Census Commissioner Dr. M. Vijayanunni estimates that India is adding 30 people to its population every minute (which adds up to 1,800 every hour—more than 15 million every year).

Unlike China, India has not turned its vast population into factory and farm workers. As many as 100 million Indians are unemployed or underemployed. Also unlike the Chinese, India's leaders did not see the population bomb coming, or they shut their eyes to it if they did. The Chinese delayed the inevitable for a considerable period by rigorously enforcing population control. But in a chaotic democracy like India, Chinese-style enforcement is not possible. The net result is that India will continue to add the equivalent of Switzerland to its population every year well into the next century. According to Vijayanunni's projections, the population will double in the next 25 years.

Pakistan's 130 million are expected to grow to 160 million in 2005 and to double by 2025. Although the abject poverty seen in India is not now present in Pakistan, it will be soon if present trends are any indication.

Indian policy-makers understandably choose to emphasize the country's impressive economic progress. They point out that India is the world's tenth largest industrial country and the second-biggest developer of computer software after the United States.

But there is a darker reality. The number of people living below what the World Bank calls the "poverty line," people who earn less than the equivalent of $1 a day, is at least 400 million. That figure significantly diminishes the value of the statistics that Indian political and business leaders like to cite—that the country's middle class, who, for example, can increasingly afford cars, now numbers around 150 million.

One group of Indian politicians, particularly in the most populous regions of north-central India, do not view the population as an economic or social handicap, but as a mammoth voting bloc. Perversely enough, the poverty that results from rampant population growth offers Indian politicians a potent rallying cry at election time: "Garibi hatao!" they shout ("Get rid of poverty!").

In Pakistan, the Islamic clergy views population control as un-Islamic. Family planning is at best a passive exercise. The net effect is that the numbers keep growing and resources become scarcer.

In 1999, the latest World Bank report on poverty indicated that the numbers of poor in South Asia had risen substantially since the last census in 1994. Although the rise in poverty cannot be ascribed to the nuclear tests or the arms race, it certainly could be linked to the decline in investment, stagnation in the job market, and the curtailment of poverty-alleviation programs, all of which have been exacerbated by the test blasts. The poverty report, released in June 1999, predicts that by 2025 South Asia will have the greatest number of people living in poverty anywhere in the world.

In that tragedy, the India-Pakistan arms race will have played its part.

The Persistence of the Indo-Pakistani Conflict

By Alexander Evans

Alexander Evans is a research associate in the Center for Defense Studies at King's College in London and the director of studies at the center for the Study of Financial Innovation. He has been studying the politics of Jammu and Kashmir (the Indian-controlled portion of Kashmir) since 1993 and has served as a consultant on issues pertaining to the region for various international organizations and nongovernmental organizations, including the United Nations and the Control Risks Groups. Evans argues in the following article that, while there are some reasons to be hopeful, tensions between India and Pakistan are likely to resurface because the two nations have not yet resolved their differences in Kashmir. Evans also illustrates the key role that the United States and Britain played in keeping a terrorist attack on the Indian Parliament in December 2001 from leading to a fourth war between the two South Asian nuclear powers.

On Thursday, December 13, 2001, five militants armed with automatic weapons and grenades stormed the Indian parliament building in New Delhi. Equipped with a false security pass and an official car of the kind often used by high-ranking politicians, they managed to make their way into the parliament courtyard. Once inside, they dashed out of the vehicle and moved toward the main parliament entrance, firing as they went. Security forces managed to restore order, but not before 14 people—including all five assailants—were killed. It was one of the most serious terrorist attacks to take place in the Indian capital. Although no group claimed responsibility, the Indians blamed two extremist militant organizations

Alexander Evans, "India, Pakistan, and the Prospect of War," *Current History*, vol. 101, April 2002, pp. 160–65.

based in Pakistan, the Jaish-e-Muhammad (Army of the Prophet) and Lashkar-e-Taiba (Army of the Pure) for the attack. Within weeks it would become the critical event that could lead to war.

The Indian prime minister, Atal Vajpayee, spoke to the Indian nation live on television. "This was not just an attack on the building, it was a warning to the entire nation," he said. The Indian media responded in kind. The next day's newspapers were full of horror at the attack—and calls for Pakistan to end support to militants, once and for all. Pointed references were made to Israel and the United States. If these two countries could combat terrorism and take on the countries behind it, why couldn't India? India's hard-line home minister, L.K. Advani, set the tone when he said: "We will liquidate the terrorists and their sponsors whoever they are, wherever they are."

Within hours Pakistani President Pervez Musharraf had condemned the attack. He added, "I would like to convey our sympathies to the government and people of India as well as our deep condolences to the bereaved families." The attack on the Indian parliament was also condemned by United States President George W. Bush, British Foreign Secretary Jack Straw, and many other world leaders.

As the days passed, the crisis deepened. To India, it was the final straw in a series of terrorist attacks—including a suicide attack on the local Kashmir State Assembly on October 1, 2001. By December 20, the atmosphere was heated. India turned down Pakistan's request for evidence backing up New Delhi's assertion that Pakistani-backed militants were responsible for the parliament attack. This was also a rebuff to the United States, which had suggested that releasing this evidence would help reduce tension. This suggestion was not taken well in New Delhi—with Indian officials pointing out (privately) that the Americans had been equally unforthcoming in their campaign against terror.

There were unconfirmed reports of Indian troop movements close to the Pakistan border in Rajasthan. Meanwhile, President Musharraf flew to China, where he held meetings with Chinese President Jiang Zemin. China has long had warm relations with Pakistan, but in two previous Indo-Pakistani wars—in 1965 and 1971—had chosen not to intervene. While there, Musharraf slipped into combative language, accusing India of "arrogance" and engaging in knee-jerk reactions.

On the border, tensions were growing. Two Indian border guards were killed on December 22, allegedly by Pakistani fire. In New Delhi, Mohammad Sharif Khan, a Pakistani diplomat, was allegedly detained and beaten by Indian security officials. Khan was accused of spying, but whether he was spying (or not) or was beaten (or not), this incident further undermined already weak diplomatic channels between India and Pakistan. The next two days saw moves by Pakistan to stave off Indian action. On December 24, the State Bank of Pakistan froze Lashkar-e-Taiba bank accounts (at the instruction of the Pakistani government). This was followed quickly the next day by the detention by Pakistani security forces of Jaish-e-Muhammad chief Maulana Masood Azhar.

But by December 25, war looked inevitable. Heavy Indian troop deployments along the Pakistani border were now accompanied by mass evacuations of civilians from adjoining areas. Indian and Pakistani forces secured their positions, laying extensive minefields in recently vacated fields and villages. Accidents on both sides linked to the transport of mines and munitions began to claim military and civilian lives.

On December 26, the United States again tried to reduce the political temperature when Secretary of State Colin Powell announced that the two militant groups India blamed for the parliament attack had been formally placed on the United States' list of banned terrorist organizations. At the same time, Pakistani intelligence suggested that India was now poised to invade Pakistan; most of its army, and almost all its air force, was deployed in an offensive formation aimed at Pakistan.

India continued to apply pressure and took a series of steps on December 27, including announcing that it would halve its diplomatic representation in Pakistan, forbid Pakistani planes to enter Indian airspace beginning January 1, 2002, and close down transport links between both countries. Pakistan reciprocated.

India also prepared a list of 20 people it accused of involvement in acts of terrorism on Indian soil—and believed to be in Pakistan. On December 31, 2001, Arun Kumar Singh, a senior Indian external affairs ministry official, called in Pakistan's deputy high commissioner, Jalil Abbas Jeelani, to present him with the list. Singh then demanded that Pakistan hand over to India for trial those named on the list.

A Crisis Slowly Defused

As the new year rolled in, feverish diplomatic activity was taking place in Washington, D.C., and London. British Prime Minister Tony Blair, it was announced, would soon travel to South Asia to meet directly with Indian and Pakistani leaders. While Britain and the United States were worried about the threat of direct conflict, they were also keen to head off the impact the crisis was beginning to have on the American-led coalition against terrorism. With work still to be done in Afghanistan, and unconfirmed reports that senior Taliban and Al

Qaeda members might be slipping away into Pakistan itself, keeping Pakistan focused on supporting the war on terror was an important foreign policy priority. Already Pakistan had moved forces to the border with India that could have been used to intercept and detain suspected terrorists entering from Afghanistan.

The onus was on Pakistan to make concessions. On January 4, 2002, the Pakistani police raided a number of locations, mainly in Punjab province, detaining militants from the Lashkar-e-Taiba and the Jaish-e-Muhammad. But Colin Powell continued to apply pressure from the American side, saying that he expected Musharraf to do more. American officials were worried that India was determined to see major Pakistani concessions, and that nothing less would assuage New Delhi's leaders.

The Indian and Pakistani leaders themselves had assembled in the Nepalese capital, Kathmandu. A long-planned regional summit of leaders from the South Asian Association for Regional Cooperation, the weak South Asian regional body established in 1985, had begun a few days before. Musharraf and Vajpayee arrived on January 4, and considerable discussion ensued as to whether they would exchange words—or even a glance—during the summit. Musharraf arrived late, leading to speculation in the Indian press that he had no intention of taking the summit seriously.

Musharraf seized the diplomatic high ground—and the photo opportunity—when he walked over to Vajpayee and offered the startled Indian prime minister his hand. Vajpayee took it, and the summit handshake added weight to Musharraf's offer, made a few hours before, of a Pakistan "hand of friendship" to India. When Vajpayee addressed the summit, however, he made it clear that India stood by its position that only concrete action from Pakistan would pave the way for normalization of relations. The only positive sign came, once more, from the media advisers, who ensured that Vajpayee reciprocated Musharraf's visual gesture at the close of the summit. Two handshakes—but no serious talks—later, both leaders headed for home.

In both cases their next international engagement was with the British prime minister. Blair had a difficult role to play. He needed to affirm British support for India in cracking down on terrorism and soothe Indian concerns about the links between Washington and Islamabad that had been renewed with the United States–led coalition attack on Afghanistan. Even before he touched down on Indian soil, Blair clarified that he would not be telling either country how to run its affairs. Blair told reporters that, while Britain had no magic formula for peace, both he and President Bush were determined to prevent war from breaking out.

Blair flew into New Delhi the following day and met with the Indian prime minister on January 6, 2002. They signed a joint declaration condemning terrorism and those who support it. And in a joint press conference the following day, Blair was careful not to endorse the specifics of Indian demands on Pakistan—although he again used language that endeared him to his Indian hosts. "The terrorist attacks of eleventh September, first October, and thirteenth December were deliberate attempts to shatter the peace of our peoples and to undermine democratic values. The attack on the Indian parliament was an attack on democracy worldwide" read the joint declaration. India's wounded national pride was given its due by the visiting British prime minister.

On January 7, 2002, Blair turned to playing to a Pakistani audience. His meeting with President Musharraf was private, and officials unofficially suggested that Blair had been blunt about what Pakistan needed to do—although warm in his gratitude for Pakistan's support in the war in Afghanistan. The press conference afterward said it all. A quiet Musharraf and a tired Blair fielded questions from the world's media. Musharraf condemned terrorism, but avoided commenting on Indian demands. He said that he had stressed to Blair Pakistan's "policy of restraint and responsibility." Blair made his views clear. There was, he said, no likelihood of international intervention to solve the Kashmir dispute—a blunt remark that did not appear on either the official Pakistani- or British-edited transcripts. And the same day India and Pakistan were again trading diplomatic brickbats, with India claiming it had shot down a Pakistani drone in Indian airspace (Pakistan denied the charge).

What did the Blair mission achieve? The British press was critical, perhaps following accusations by the opposition Conservative Party that Blair was neglecting domestic priorities. One or two commentators acerbically noted that Blair was also encouraging India to buy British-manufactured Hawk jets, a role that sat uneasily with his mission for peace. But Blair helped convey an important message from New Delhi (and Washington) to Pakistan—that the regime in Islamabad needed to respond substantively to Indian demands—while keeping India informed. Both the United States and Britain tilted toward India throughout the crisis to keep India from military action (Indian action could have provoked a nuclear exchange between the two recently declared nuclear powers, especially if Pakistan felt close to collapse following an Indian assault).

Following Blair's departure from Pakistan, the Pakistani administration again was keen to keep the United States involved. On January 8, 2002, it became public knowledge that the government of Pakistan would allow American forces to enter Pakistani territory in "hot pursuit" of escaping terrorist suspects. Pakistan also formally detained the Lashkar-e-Taiba's supreme leader, Hafiz Muhammad Saeed. . . .

India's Gamble

India seized an opportunity in December 2001. In escalating a crisis into a global drama, Prime Minister Vajpayee and his colleagues took a calculated risk. A sharp deterioration in Indo-Pakistani relations was to be expected, but the massive military buildup that followed was optional. Indian officials sensed a brief window of opportunity, and put together a strategy to make the most of it. The Indian public came on board, not least because the direct nature of the attack on the Indian parliament resonated with American shock at the September 11 terror attacks. Yet the policy was not driven by Indian public opinion; differences between elements in the ruling Bharatiya Janata Party–led coalition were more important. . . .

Musharraf has accepted Indian demands that he act against extremist militant groups operating from Pakistan. His country has been portrayed as a safe harbor for terrorists, and one in which action is only belatedly being taken. Even so, Musharraf has managed to take back much of the presentational territory lost in the December 13, 2001, suicide attack on the Indian parliament. By boldly setting out a fresh path for Pakistan—with support from his fellow generals—he may achieve more than many of his elected, civilian predecessors. Ironically, Musharraf may have seized a series of small victories from an apparent diplomatic defeat in January 2002. He has earned United States praise for responding to Indian demands. He has traded in extremist groups (who opposed him anyway), but has kept open lines with the Hezb-ul Mujahedeen. In Pakistan itself, he has renewed a national vision. It is not enough, though, for him to attempt to eliminate sectarianism and regulate foreign students (who are sometimes militant) resident in Pakistan. He faces several major challenges, all of which will need sustained action, not just words, to overcome.

Pakistan's economy and institutions are in a poor state. The additional aid, both bilateral and multilateral, that has flowed into the country since it joined the international coalition against terror—$1 billion from the United States alone—is only a stop-gap. The country's creditors agreed to restructure $12.5 billion of the country's external debt in December 2001, and fresh loans have been promised.

But funds alone cannot solve Pakistan's crisis of governance; only a strengthening of Pakistan's institutions, action against corruption, and a collective commitment from the nation's elite will alter the trend of previous decades. If Pakistan is to prosper, Musharraf must offer more than words. And democracy, barely mentioned since Pakistan recovered its position as a significant United States ally, must form a part of the equation. To be fair, Musharraf has not been an old-school dictator, replete with dubious dress-sense and an insatiable appetite for power. Instead, he took on the reins of government almost reluctantly in October 1999, displacing former Prime Minister Nawaz Sharif's disintegrating and corrupt administration. Musharraf says he will return Pakistan to democracy—and it looks as if he means it, unlike Pakistan's last military dictator, General Zia ul-Haq, whose rule only ended with his death in 1988. Pakistan's new friendship with the United States—assuming it can last—can help steer it into safe waters as it pursues a return to democracy.

America's Role

The December 2001 crisis showed how critical the American role is in South Asia. United Nations efforts to forge a peaceful settlement foundered; while India welcomes functional UN bodies (like UNCTAD and UNESCO), it is directly opposed to a UN role in settling South Asian disputes. Direct intervention by the United States or Britain is also rejected—but Washington can use good offices to help tamp down tensions.

How did the United States intervene during this latest crisis? Washington conducted an open and a private campaign to encourage India to back down from open conflict, all the time encouraging Pakistan to take steps against its own militants. President Bush also personally announced the banning of the Lashkar-e-Taiba on December 21, 2001, calling it a "stateless sponsor of terrorism." His statement signaled America's commitment to take a stand against groups determined to exacerbate Indo-Pakistani hostility. And when Musharraf finally conceded to some of India's demands, American leaders were quick to praise him.

America has intensified its efforts to reduce regional tension by restraining India and encouraging concessions from Pakistan. In the future it needs to focus on Kashmir, which is the proximate cause of Indo-Pakistani tension. The Kashmir issue must be solved—or at least salved. The United States has tried to do so before, each time failing to deliver a peaceful compromise acceptable to India and Pakistan. In the 1950s, American efforts were largely directed through the UN, failing mainly due to the Indians. In the early 1960s, an intensive bilateral effort involving six rounds of Indo-Pakistani talks yielded little, largely in the face of Pakistani obstruction. Since the 1965 Indo-Pakistani war the United States has shied away from active attempts to solve the Kashmir dispute, while keeping open the offer of its good offices should India and Pakistan jointly seek to call on them.

Future Tensions, Future Hopes

Another South Asian crisis has apparently subsided. But with no clear sign of improved relations between India and Pakistan, tensions are bound to bubble to the surface once more.

Three facts give cause for optimism. First, the crisis has not become a war—as it easily could have on December 29, 2001. Second, in late February 2002 the border between India and Pakistan was remarkably quiet. After a surfeit of cross-border shelling and occasional displays of machismo, the message on both sides appears to be restraint. Third, Pakistan has reviewed its Kashmir policy by banning the two major militant groups, the Lashkar-e-Taiba and the Jaish-e-Muhammad, and by showing a willingness to address sectarian strife—and international militants. Pakistan thus appears to have prevented Indian military action.

There are also three reasons for pessimism. First, India and Pakistan have not resolved their differences—which remain vast. The organizing principles of Pakistan's Kashmir policy continue to challenge Indian claims to sovereignty in Kashmir. And, on a regular basis, senior Indians continue to use strong language—for example, talking of an "axis of terror" (to echo President Bush's State of the Union address regarding Iraq, Iran, and North Korea) based in Pakistan. Reduced diplomatic links make misperception and renewed sources of tension likely.

Second, both countries remain at a high level of military mobilization—an expensive and possibly dangerous state of affairs. High concentrations of military forces, mines, and borders do not mix well. The lack of significant demobilization points to continuing concerns in New Delhi that Indian diplomatic objectives have not yet been met. And third, there is a wildcard. Most militants have fallen into line behind Musharraf, but a radical tail retains the capacity to strike at Indian targets—and lacks the constraint of Pakistani support to hold them back from attacks like that on the Indian parliament. For example, militants from the banned Lashkar-e-Taiba have reformed themselves, mounting a campaign to disprove their terrorist status and stating that they will not target Westerners in an attempt to gain Islamabad's favor, but elements in the Jaish-e-Muhammad have vowed to continue their war—with or without Pakistani support.

One member of this radical tail is surely the suspected terrorist Ahmed Sheikh. A one-time student at the London School of Economics, he has already been involved in one kidnapping (of American and British backpackers in India in 1994). Although he was arrested by India in connection with that case, he was then released as part of a deal with the hijackers of an Indian Airlines flight in December 1999. Slipping back into Pakistan, he went deep underground.

On January 23, 2002, Daniel Pearl, an American journalist with the *Wall Street Journal*, disappeared while pursuing a story in Karachi, Pakistan. He was kidnapped by unknown militants, probably connected to Ahmed Sheikh. Although Sheikh was arrested by Pakistani authorities on February 12, 2002, at some stage Pearl was murdered—and his videotaped death was confirmed on February 21, 2002. Pearl was a victim of the same sectarianism that has ripped apart Pakistan since the early 1980s—a sectarianism that makes simplistic assertions about religion and politics (one of the putative reasons given for Pearl's kidnap was that he was a Jew).

An equally deformed politics shapes relations between India and Pakistan. When thinking about each other, both nations are obsessed with the past and blind to their own current domestic problems. In his January 2002 speech, President Musharraf made a start by promising to take on Pakistan's extremists. He will be judged by his actions. In India, the festering problem of Kashmir requires political as well as military attention—and it is not clear whether the Indian government has the will or the desire to rectify past wrongs and engage with ordinary Kashmiris. As one sign of progress, India has appointed a new representative to advance a process of dialogue in Kashmir. The official, Wajahat Habibullah, a Muslim Indian bureaucrat, is well respected on all sides and could make headway, despite expectations to the contrary.

There continues to be ample scope for tension between these two hostile neighbors. India still harbors doubts about Pakistan's commitment to peace, and Pakistani policymakers remain anxious about Indian policies, wondering whether the threat of war may be used again. Unfortunately, the precedent suggests that a measure of military threat helped deliver Indian diplomatic objectives. Fortunately, Pakistan's response to the crisis suggests that its covert war on India in Kashmir may soon be reined in. Can violence—and the threat of violence—ever be removed from Indo-Pakistani relations?

An Argument for Kashmiri Independence

By Ziauddin Sardar

Ziauddin Sardar is a writer and cultural critic who serves as a visiting pro-
fessor of post-colonial studies at the City University in London and is the ed-
itor of Futures: The Monthly Journal of Policy, Planning, and Future Studies.
In the following excerpt, Sardar describes the tense relations between India
and Pakistan caused by the Kashmir issue, which he states is likely to be the
source of the next "world-shattering conflict." Sardar also argues that the
scenario of a nuclear war between India and Pakistan in the event of conflict
is likely because the leaders of both nations have strong incentives to use their
nuclear arsenals. According to Sardar, the best way for India and Pakistan
to resolve their differences and reduce the threat of a nuclear war in South
Asia might be to give Kashmir its independence.

S pare a thought for the Taj Mahal. The wondrous 17th-century
monument to love shines like a beacon on moonlit nights, making it an incongruous and conspicuous landmark at a time when India and Pakistan are poised for war. So the Taj is to be covered with
camouflage cloth as a precaution against Pakistani air space raids.
But if there is a fourth war between the two siblings (even after Tony
Blair's peacemaking mission to the Indian subcontinent), more than
the Taj Mahal needs protecting. The likeliest end to such a conflict
would be a nuclear exchange. This cataclysmic risk is almost taken
for granted in Pakistani military circles. And it is also the conclusion reached by various military thinkers and strategists in the
United States.

Between 2000 and 2002, US think-tanks conducted a number of

studies simulating a new war between India and Pakistan. In these "war games", military commentators and academics play the parts of leaders on each side. In almost nine out of ten cases, these simulations ended with nuclear war. Indeed, the escalation of tension in late 2001—with nuclear missiles deployed on each side and Indian warships moving close to Karachi, Pakistan's largest city and only port—was a carbon copy of standard war-game scenarios that end with a nuclear exchange.

The cold-blooded rationale behind this scenario goes something like this. India, the fourth-largest military power in the world, with armed forces twice the size of Pakistan's, could outgun its neighbour. Karachi and Lahore, Pakistan's main cultural centre located relatively close to the border, are particularly vulnerable. To save these cities, Pakistan launches a nuclear strike. Precisely because neither side has very many nuclear weapons, there is a strong incentive to launch the first strike. It is simply a case of "use it or lose it".

The rhetoric on both sides hints at these possibilities. When Pakistan's leader, General Pervez Musharraf, warned India that "any misadventure" would result in "tremendous casualties", he was clearly referring to the nuclear endgame. India's foolishly hawkish defence minister, George Fernandes, replied: "Pakistan would be finished. We could take a strike, survive and then hit back." Because of the paucity of their nuclear arsenals, neither side is restrained by the certainty of mutually assured destruction (MAD). Instead, jingoistic lobbies on both sides indulge in macho posturing which betrays a complete disregard for the destruction and suffering that any nuclear exchange would inflict upon their peoples.

On the Brink of War

Relations between the two neighbours deteriorated after the attack on the Indian parliament in Delhi on 13 December 2001, in which 14 people died, including the five suicide attackers. India blamed the attack on the Kashmiri militant group Lashkar-e-Toiba and accused Pakistan of sponsoring terrorist groups. It demanded that Pakistan take harsh measures against them. Hafiz Mohammad Saeed, a leader of Lashkar-e-Toiba, was arrested.

That Pakistan's intelligence service supported and ecouraged the Kashmiri militants is no secret. Together with the al-Qaeda terrorists, the militants have been trained in the religious seminaries of northern Pakistan, which have become the bedrock of fundamentalism in the region. If General Musharraf is serious about his promises to restore a moderate Pakistan, he will have to close down the religious seminaries.

Behind the warmongering on the other side lurks the Hindu nationalists' dream of a pure Hindu India—"Akhand Bharat"—where orthodox "Hindu Dharma" is the creed of all, and where everyone— women, the untouchables and other "lower" caste groups—knows his or her place in society. Above all, the dream is of an India free from the "Muslim invaders".

Since the ascent to power of the Bharatiya Janata Party (BJP), numerous attempts have been made to write Islam out of India's history books. If the valorous high-caste Hindus had been true to their creed, these revisionist texts suggest, they would have destroyed the Moguls, defeated the Muslims, and driven out the British with blood and chivalry.

The BJP Hindu government has projected the nuclear tests of May 1998 as signs of Hindu reawakening. Nuclear weapons are being romanticised as symbols of indigenous Vedic strength and virility, whose purpose, as the home minister, LK Advani, has declared, is to "teach Muslims and Pakistan a lesson". Little wonder that the openly nationalist prime minister, Atal Behari Vajpayee, views the current crisis as an opportunity to settle old scores. First he talked of crossing the border into Pakistan to destroy the terrorist camps. Then he wanted to emulate "Bush in Afghanistan" or "Israel in Palestine". Now he has moved most of the Indian army, complete with nuclear missiles, to the borders of Pakistan. Yet Pakistan is in the "nuclear club", and India must learn to treat its neighbour as an equal partner.

Indian officials who talk of "whacking Pakistan" as though it were on a par with insolvent Afghanistan or the helpless Palestinians risk making a devastating mistake. And the Hindu chauvinist fantasy of "finishing Pakistan" is just that—a perilous fantasy. Moreover, India cannot duck the Kashmir issue for much longer.

Kashmiri Independence and Peace in South Asia

Kashmir, even more than the Middle East, looms as the next worldshattering conflict. As an overwhelmingly Muslim province, Kashmir should have acceded to Pakistan. But its Maharaja Hari Singh, ignoring the wishes of his people, preferred to side with India. The accession to India, as spelt out by the last British governor-general, Lord Mountbatten, was to be the subject of a free and impartial plebiscite; but India has systematically refused to hold a referendum—despite various UN resolutions. Today, India and Pakistan divide the control of Kashmir between them—though the Muslim population of Kashmir has been rising against Indian occupation for decades. Since the early 1990s, India has stationed up to 700,000 troops within Kashmir to try to quell the rebellion.

Given that independent observers have documented countless atrocities carried out by the Indian military against the Kashmiri population, it seems disingenuous of India to pretend that the crisis in Kashmir is the work of terrorists, or of a covertly hostile Pakistan.

The Kashmiris, I suspect, do not want to be governed by Pakistan, any more than they desire to live under Indian rule. And indeed, it is about time that the two feuding subcontinental siblings took seriously the idea of an independent Kashmir. Discussion of reuniting the country as an autonomous buffer zone might offer a way out for everyone. This way, the two neighbouring states could channel some of the millions they spend on their military arsenals to meeting the needs of their citizens.

The lustrous glow of the Taj Mahal—the mausoleum built by the Mogul emperor Shah Jahan for his beloved wife Mumtaz Mahal in the northern Indian city of Agra—illuminates the shared history of the peoples of India and Pakistan.

A Muslim monument in an Indian city, the Taj remains a stunning testament to mutual cultural influences; these influences must not be camouflaged. Lasting peace on the subcontinent depends on recovering the dynamism that used to characterise this complex fusion, not obscuring—or, worse, obliterating—it with rabid nationalism.

CHAPTER 3

Pakistan and the War on Terror

Pakistan Must Join the War on Terror

By Pervez Musharraf

Pervez Musharraf was born in Delhi, India, in 1943 to a well-educated Muslim family. After the creation of Pakistan, Musharraf's father moved his family to Karachi. Musharraf joined the Pakistan Military Academy in 1961 and became a highly decorated officer after serving in the 1965 and 1971 wars with India. As chief of army staff, he engineered a tactically brilliant, but politically disastrous, assault on Indian forces in the Kashmiri town of Kargil in the spring of 1999. After being fired for his efforts in Kargil by Prime Minister Nawaz Sharif, Musharraf led a bloodless coup against Sharif and declared himself chief executive on October 12, 1999. The following selection is a speech Musharraf delivered to Pakistani radio and television audiences on September 19, 2001, explaining his decision to join the American-led War on Terror. Musharraf claimed joining the war was necessary to maintain Pakistan's sovereignty, to protect its nuclear arsenal, and to advance its interests in Kashmir.

The situation confronting the nation today and the international crisis have impelled me to take the nation into confidence.

First of all, I would like to express heartfelt sympathies to the United States for the thousands of valuable lives lost in the United States due to horrendous acts of terrorism.

We are all the more grieved because in this incident people from about 45 countries from all over the world lost their lives. People of all ages, children, women and people from all and every religion lost their lives. Many Pakistanis also lost their lives.

These people were capable Pakistanis who had gone to improve their lives. On this loss of lives I express my sympathies with those families. I pray to Allah to rest their souls in peace.

This act of terrorism has raised a wave of deep grief, anger and re-

Pervez Musharraf, "Address by General Pervez Musharraf, President of Pakistan, Delivered as a Broadcast on Radio and Television from Islamabad on September 19, 2001," *Vital Speeches of the Day*, vol. 67, October 1, 2001, pp. 754–56.

taliation in the United States. Their first target from day one is Osama bin Laden's movement Al-Qaida about which they say that it is their first target.

The second target are Taliban and that is because Taliban have given refuge to Osama and his network. This has been their demand for many years.

They have been demanding their extradition and presentation before the international court of justice. Taliban have been rejecting this. The third target is a long war against terrorism at the international level. The thing to ponder is that in these three targets nobody is talking about war against Islam or the people of Afghanistan.

Pakistan is being asked to support this campaign. What is this support? Generally speaking, there are three important things in which America is asking for our help.

First is intelligence and information exchange, second support is the use of our airspace and the third is that they are asking for logistic support from us.

I would like to tell you now that they do not have any operational plan right now. Therefore we do not have any details on this count but we know that whatever are the United States' intentions they have the support of the U.N. Security Council and the General Assembly in the form of a resolution.

This is a resolution for war against terrorism and this is a resolution for punishing those people who support terrorism. Islamic countries have supported this resolution. This is the situation as it prevailed in the outside world.

Now I would like to inform you about the internal situation. Pakistan is facing a very critical situation and I believe that after 1971, this is the most critical period. The decision we take today can have far-reaching and wide-ranging consequences. The crisis is formidable and unprecedented. If we take wrong decisions in this crisis, it can lead to worse consequences. On the other hand, if we take right decisions, its results will be good. The negative consequences can endanger Pakistan's integrity and solidarity. Our critical concerns, our important concerns can come under threat. When I say critical concerns, I mean our strategic assets and the cause of Kashmir. If these come under threat it would be a worse situation for us.

On the other hand, we can re-emerge politically as a responsible and dignified nation and all our difficulties can be minimized. I have considered all these factors and held consultations with those who hold different opinions. I met the corps commanders, National Security Council and the Federal Cabinet. I interacted with the media. I invited the religious scholars and held discussions with them. I met politicians. I also invited intellectuals. I will be meeting with the tribal chiefs and Kashmiri leaders tomorrow. This is the same process of consultation that I held earlier.

I noted that there was difference of opinion but an overwhelming majority favours patience, prudence and wisdom. Some of them, I think about ten percent, favoured a sentimental approach.

Let us now take a look at the designs of our neighbouring country [India]. They offered all their military facilities to the United States. They have offered without hesitation, all their facilities, all their bases and full logistic support. They want to enter into any alliance with the Unites States and get Pakistan declared a terrorist state.

They want to harm our strategic assets and the Kashmir cause. Not only this, recently certain countries met in Dushanbe. India was one of them. Indian representative was there. What do the Indians want? They do not have common borders with Afghanistan anywhere. It is totally isolated from Afghanistan.

In my view, it would not be surprising, that the Indians want to ensure that if and when the government in Afghanistan changes, it shall be an anti-Pakistan government.

It is very important that while the entire world is talking about this horrible terrorist attack, our neighbouring country instead of talking peace and cooperation, was trying hard to harm Pakistan and defame Islam. If you watch their television, you will find them dishing out propaganda against Pakistan, day in and day out. I would like to tell India "Lay Off."

Pakistan's armed forces and every Pakistani citizen is ready to offer any sacrifice in order to defend Pakistan and secure its strategic assets. Make no mistake and entertain no misunderstanding. At this very moment our Air Force is at high alert; and they are ready for "Do or die" missions. My countrymen! In such a situation, a wrong decision can lead to unbearable losses.

What are our critical concerns and priorities? These are four:

First of all is the security of the country and external threat.

Second is our economy and its revival.

Third are our strategic nuclear and missile assets.

And the Kashmir cause.

The four are our critical concerns. Any wrong judgement on our part can damage all our interests. While taking a decision, we have to keep in mind all these factors.

The decision should reflect supremacy of righteousness and it should be in conformity with Islam. Whatever we are doing, it is according to Islam and it upholds the principle of righteousness. I would like to say that decisions about the national interests should be made with wisdom and rational judgement.

At this moment, it is not the question of bravery or cowardice. We are all very brave. My own response in such situations is usually of daring. But bravery without rational judgement tantamounts to stupidity. There is no clash between bravery and sound judgement.

Allah Almighty says in the holy Quran, "The one bestowed with sagacity is the one who gets a big favour from Allah." We have to take recourse to sanity. We have to save our nation from damage. We have to build up our national respect. "Pakistan comes first, everything else comes later."

Some scholars and religious leaders are inclined towards taking emotional decisions. I would like to remind them the events of the first six years of the history of Islam.

The Islamic calendar started from migration. The significance of migration is manifested from the fact that the Holy Prophet went from Makkah to Madinah. He migrated to safeguard Islam.

What was migration? God forbid, was it an act of cowardice? The Holy Prophet signed the charter of Madinah (Meesaq-e-Madinah) with the Jewish tribes. It was an act of sagacity.

This treaty remained effective for six years. Three battles were fought with non-believers of Makkah during this period—the battle of Badr, Uhad and Khandaq. The Muslims emerged victorious in these battles with the non-believers of Makkah because the Jews had signed a treaty with the Muslims.

After six years, the Jews were visibly disturbed with the progress of Islam, which was getting stronger and stronger. They conspired to forge covert relations with the non-believers of Makkah.

Realising the danger, the Holy Prophet signed the treaty of Hudaibiya with the Makkhans who had been imposing wars on Islam. This was a no war pact.

I would like to draw your attention to one significant point of this pact. The last portion of the pact was required to be signed by the Holy Prophet as Muhammad Rasool Allah.

The non-believers contested that they did not recognize Muhammad as the Prophet of Allah. They demanded to erase these words from the text of the treaty. The Holy Prophet agreed but Hazrat Umar protested against it. He got emotional and asked the Holy Prophet if he was not the messenger of God (God forbid) and whether the Muslims were not on the right path while signing the treaty.

The Holy Prophet advised Hazrat Umar not to be led by emotions as the dictates of national thinking demanded signing of the treaty at that time. He said, this was advantageous to Islam and as years would pass by you would come to know of its benefits. This is exactly what happened. Six months later in the battle of Khyber, Muslims, by the grace of Allah, again became victorious. It should be remembered that this became possible because Makkhans could not attack because of the treaty. On 8 Hijra by the grace of Allah glory of Islam spread to Makkah.

What is the lesson for us in this? The lesson is that when there is a crisis situation, the path of wisdom is better than the path of emotions. Therefore, we have to take a strategic decision.

There is no question of weakness of faith or cowardice. For Pakistan, life can be sacrificed and I am sure every Pakistani will give his life for Pakistan. I have fought two wars. I have seen dangers. I faced them and by the grace of Allah never committed a cowardly act.

But at this time one should not bring harm to the country. We cannot make the future of a hundred and forty million people bleak. Even otherwise it is said in Shariah that if there are two difficulties at a time and a selection has to be made it is better to opt for the lesser one. Some of our friends seem to be much worried about Afghanistan.

I must tell them that I and my government are much more worried about Afghanistan and Taliban. I have done everything for Afghanistan and Taliban when the entire world is against them. I have met about twenty to twenty-five world leaders and talked to each of them in favour of the Taliban. I have told them that sanctions should not be imposed on Afghanistan and that we should engage them.

I have been repeating this stance before all leaders but I am sorry to say that none of our friends accepted this.

Even in this situation, we are trying our best to cooperate with them. I sent the Director General of the Inter-Services Intelligence (ISI) with my personal letter to Mullah Umar [the leader of the Taliban]. He returned after spending two days there. I have informed Mullah Umar about the gravity of the situation. We are trying our best to come out of this critical situation without any damage to Afghanistan and Taliban. This is my earnest endeavour and with the blessings of Allah I will continue to seek such a way out. We are telling the Americans too that they should be patient. Whatever their plans, they should be cautious and balanced: We are asking them to come up with whatever evidence they have against Osama bin Laden. What I would like to know is how do we save Afghanistan and Taliban. And how do we ensure that they suffer minimum losses: I am sure that you will favour that we do so and bring some improvement by working with the nations of the world. At this juncture, I am worried about Pakistan only.

I am the Supreme Commander of Pakistan and I give top priority to the defence of Pakistan. Defence of any other country comes later. We want to take decisions in the interest of Pakistan. I know that the majority of the people favour our decisions. I also know that some elements are trying to take unfair advantage of the situation and promote their personal agenda and advance the interests of their parties. They are poised to create dissentions and damage the country.

There is no reason why this minority should be allowed to hold the sane majority as a hostage. I appeal to all Pakistanis to display unity and solidarity and foil the nefarious designs of such elements who intend to harm the interests of the country.

At this critical juncture, we have to frustrate the evil designs of our enemies and safeguard national interests. Pakistan is considered a fortress of Islam. God forbid, if this fortress is harmed in any way it would cause damage to the cause of Islam. My dear countrymen, have trust in me the way you reposed trust in me before going to Agra. I did not disappoint the nation there.

We have not compromised on national honour and integrity and I shall not disappoint you on this occasion either. This is a firm pledge to you. In the end before I take your leave, I would like to end with the prayer of Hazrat Musa (Prophet Moses) as given in Sura-e-Taha: "May Allah open my chest, make my task easier, untie my tongue so that they may comprehend my intent."

May Allah be with us in our endeavours.

The United States Should Assist Pakistan in Exchange for Its Support in the War on Terror

By Dennis Kux

Dennis Kux is a former South Asia specialist for the U.S. State Department and a former diplomat to India and Pakistan, having served three different times in each country. He has recently published a book on American-Pakistani relations and is serving as a senior scholar for the Woodrow Wilson International Center for Scholars. In this selection, Kux describes what he refers to as the "Islamization" of Pakistani society that has contributed to sectarian violence and religious fundamentalism, both of which threatened the government of Pervez Musharraf in the aftermath of his decision to support the American war effort in Afghanistan. According to Kux, America must aid the economy to help stabilize the situation inside Pakistan and to protect its own security interests in the region. In addition, Kux cautions against the United States helping Pakistan with military aid because it can be used for undesirable purposes—such as supporting insurgents in Kashmir—that the United States must discourage if it is to successfully prosecute its War on Terror.

On September 10, 2001, Pakistan was a country of secondary interest to the United States. Although it had been America's "most allied ally in Asia" in the 1950s and an indispensable partner in the struggle against the Soviets in Afghanistan in the 1980s, the relationship unraveled after the Soviets pulled out of Afghanistan. In October 1990, the United States suspended economic and military aid under the Pressler amendment because Pakistan had developed nuclear weapons. Its May 1998 nuclear tests and the army's overthrow of the civilian government of Nawaz Sharif in October 1999 led to further sanctions against the one-time U.S. ally.

Thus, when President Bill Clinton touched down for five hours in Islamabad on March 25, 2000—the first journey to Pakistan by a U.S. chief executive in more than thirty years—the mood was tense, and contrasted sharply with his highly successful five-day visit to India. In their talks, Clinton and General Pervez Musharraf, Pakistan's military dictator, differed over major issues: how best to deal with the fundamentalist Taliban in Afghanistan and other Islamic extremists; how best to deal with the Kashmir dispute; a timetable for the return of democracy; and nuclear weapons issues. Clinton outlined his concerns to Musharraf in a frank but conciliatory manner and then repeated them in a television address to the people of Pakistan. Out of the public spotlight, the President worried about Pakistan's chronic political instability, the growing threat of fundamentalism, its mounting economic woes and the continuing fixation on India. With the country drifting toward national failure, the worst-case fear was that, like its neighbor Afghanistan, Pakistan might be engulfed by Islamic fundamentalism. A Pakistan ruled by religious extremists and armed with nuclear weapons posed a nightmare scenario with ramifications far transcending South Asia. Amid such concerns, Clinton's inability to produce a better U.S. relationship with Pakistan inevitably left the impression that the United States was "tilting" toward India.

The incoming Bush Administration picked up where Clinton left off, this despite the Cold War tradition of Republican warmth toward governments in Islamabad. The new leadership in Washington soon made clear that its top priority in South Asia was to continue the process of improving relations with India. Pakistan's image remained largely negative both in official Washington and in the prestige press.

The events of September 11 have changed all that. Geography and history have once more made Pakistan important to U.S. interests. Islamabad's support is required in order to deal with Osama bin Laden, his Arab terrorist colleagues in Al-Qaeda and their Taliban hosts. Pakistan's long common frontier with Afghanistan, the intimate ethnic links between Pashtuns on both sides of the border, and the in-depth knowledge that Pakistan's intelligence service has of its neighbor make Islamabad a key partner in " bringing the terrorists to justice or justice to the terrorists", as President Bush put it on September 20, 2001. Pakistan has become pivotal. . . .

The Islamization of Pakistan

Pakistani society itself has changed. What has happened in Pakistan is not so much its "Talibanization", as some have claimed, as its Islamization. This development began in the late-1970s when President Muhammad Zia ul-Haq sought to gain greater political legitimacy for his unpopular rule by making Islam a central feature of Pakistani life. Although Pakistan was created to provide a homeland for the Muslims of India, its founding fathers, Mohammed Ali Jinnah and Liaquat Ali Khan, were secularists. They supported the idea of a separate state not for religious reasons but from fear that the Hindu majority would not respect Muslim minority rights in a united India. Until Zia took over, Pakistani leaders paid lip service to Islam but not too much more. In his Islamization policy, however, Zia substituted traditional Quranic punishments for Western legal norms, established a special *sharia* court to ensure that Pakistan's laws were consistent with the Quran, cooperated with religious parties, especially the Jamaat-i-Islami (which, ironically, had opposed the formation of Pakistan), and promoted the establishment of *madrassas.*

In the two decades since, the *madrassas* have spread widely and now number in the thousands. The government's failure to provide educational facilities, especially in rural areas, created a void that the religious schools have filled. They have produced a large subculture of youth who are lettered in the Quran but little else, and are inculcated with religious fanaticism for *jihad* against India, the United States and other alleged enemies of Islam. The Taliban are the most prominent product of the *madrassas*, but other graduates have provided the foot soldiers for several militant fundamentalist groups that have become a destabilizing feature of Pakistan's internal scene. In recent years, for example, sectarian violence between militant Sunni and Shi'a groups (the Shi'a minority constitutes 15 to 20 percent of the population) has become a serious problem, intensifying the overall sense of insecurity that has gripped the country.

Since the mid-1970s, Pakistan's military intelligence service, the Inter-Services Intelligence (ISI) has also become a much more important player both domestically and in national security policy. Established in the late 1940s, the ISI at first operated much as the CIA and other external intelligence services do, collecting intelligence and running covert operations outside the home country. Zulfikar Ali Bhutto, unhappy with the work of the internal service, the Intelligence Bureau, gave the ISI a mandate in the mid-1970s to undertake domestic operations as well as those abroad. The ISI has ever since been an active and destabilizing force in Pakistan's political life, promoting the army's agenda and opposing perceived opponents. Thus, the ISI vigorously supported Nawaz Sharif against Benazir Bhutto in the 1988 and 1990 elections.

As a result of the Afghan war, the ISI grew in both size and power. At Zia's orders, it served both as the conduit for all foreign assistance flowing to the Afghan resistance and as the planner and coordinator of *mujaheddin* activities. Covert aid from the CIA, which was matched dollar for dollar by Saudi Arabia, began rather modestly— just $30 million in 1981. By 1986, however, the total Afghan program had ballooned to more than $1 billion a year, all flowing directly through the ISI's hands.

After the Soviets left Afghanistan, the ISI continued to mastermind Pakistan's involvement in Afghanistan. Since 1994, this has meant working with and supporting the Taliban. The ISI has also had the responsibility for orchestrating *jihadi* groups active in the anti-India insurgency in Kashmir. After years of cooperation between the ISI and the militants, it is not surprising that support for fundamentalist views has gained ground within the intelligence agency. It is wrong, however, to see the ISI as an independent actor or a "rogue elephant." It takes its orders from the government, even though at times, when the lines of authority are blurred (for example, after Zia's death in 1988), it can gain more independent leeway. . . .

Musharraf's Choice

On September 11, 2001, Pervez Musharraf had been in power for 23 months. His record was mixed. The International Monetary Fund (IMF) gave good marks to Musharraf's Finance Minister Shaukat Aziz, a former Citibank official, for his efforts to clean up the country's finances. Debt relief was forthcoming, although not as much as Pakistan wanted. Development lending was extended for the first time in a number of years. Corruption had tapered off, and few alleged that Musharraf and his colleagues were lining their pockets. Still, the economy remained in the doldrums, suffering from lack of domestic investment.

Observers also accepted Musharraf's good intentions in trying to decentralize government even if they questioned the practicality of his proposed reforms. Musharraf also seemed to be serious about handing back power to elected national and provincial assemblies in the fall of 2002 as directed by Pakistan's supreme court. At the same time, he made clear that he intended to stay around. In June 2001 he pushed aside the figurehead civilian president and appointed himself president in his place (he was previously styled "the chief executive"). More recently, he re-appointed himself as Army Chief of Staff, the real seat of power in a military regime. At the same time, Musharraf left the press relatively free and did not impose martial law.

Before the events of September 11, Musharraf had made little change in Pakistan's foreign and security policies. He maintained a hardline approach toward India, continuing Pakistan's support for the insurgency in Kashmir. He also continued friendly ties with the Taliban, disregarding the global opprobrium that the Taliban earned by their outrageous conduct.

Although Musharraf has a secular outlook and is not an Islamic extremist, his government before the September 11 terrorist attacks failed to rein in the major religious parties, the Jamaat-i-Islami, the Jamiat-e-Ulema Pakistan, and the Jamiat-e-Ulema Islam (which, in particular, supported the Taliban). For example, the Musharraf government backed off from moderating Pakistan's harsh anti-blasphemy laws in the face of objections by the religious parties. It appeared, therefore, that Musharraf was content with the status quo—but that status quo begs a short description.

Despite official patronage from Zia and the ISI, the religious parties have never been able to attract mass support and have rarely gained more than five percent of the vote. The clout of the fundamentalists has come from their militancy, their ability to bring mobs into the streets and their willingness to exert pressure on the administration of the day, whether that of Benazir Bhutto, Nawaz Sharif or Pervez Musharraf. It was as if Pakistani regimes had made a Faustian bargain with the fundamentalist parties, affording them political space and legitimacy in return for their service as a vehicle to promote Pakistan's national interests, via the ISI, first in Afghanistan and more recently in Kashmir.

On September 11, the day the terrorists struck, Lt. Gen. Mahmood Ahmed, the since-replaced Director General of ISI, was in Washington on a routine liaison visit. The next day, Deputy Secretary of State Richard Armitage called him in to deliver what amounted to an ultimatum. In moving against bin Laden and other terrorists in Afghanistan, the United States wanted to know where Pakistan stood. Would it be willing to provide intelligence cooperation, allow U.S. overflights and offer logistical support? Armitage did not say what the United States would do for Pakistan in return. Secretary of State Colin Powell followed up with a phone call to Musharraf saying, in effect, that Pakistan had to choose between joining the fight against terrorism and international isolation. Unlike the Carter and Reagan Administrations of 1980 and 1981, the Bush Administration played hardball with Islamabad.

The decision was not easy for Musharraf and his senior colleagues. They realized that public opinion in the country was opposed to co-operating with the United States. Even if active backing for the Taliban and bin Laden was limited to the religious parties and their supporters, the average Pakistani did not like the idea of becoming involved in a conflict with neighboring Afghanistan and deeply distrusted Washington. Pakistanis believed their supposed U.S. ally had betrayed them not only by refusing to help in the 1965 war against India, but, even worse, by cutting off the military and economic aid on which Pakistan depended. More recently, in 1990 Pakistanis felt that after Washington no longer needed Pakistan to afflict the Soviets in Afghanistan, the United States discarded them "like a piece of used Kleenex," imposing nuclear sanctions and suspending aid, to boot.

But paradoxically, despite this disenchantment and the absence of military or significant economic help since 1990, the United States still casts a long shadow over Islamabad. Only partly in jest, Pakistanis say that their country is ruled by the three A's: Allah, the Army and America. Among the English-speaking elite—senior military officers, civil servants, rural landlords (the so-called feudals) and the business community—the American connection runs strong. They may bemoan U.S. policy, but they send their children to the United States for education and seek political, security and business links with America. Many in the elite have relatives in the 400,000-strong Pakistani-American community. Pervez Musharraf's own brother is an American citizen, a doctor in Chicago.

The average non-English speaking Pakistani tends to hold stronger anti-American views, reflecting the harder line of the Urdu-language press. The man in the street in Karachi, Lahore, Islamabad, and especially in Peshawar and Quetta, sees the United States as not just anti-Pakistani (and of late pro-Indian) but as genuinely anti-Islamic. This opinion echoes widespread, longstanding anger over U.S. policy toward Israel and the Palestinians and, more recently, over policies such as the continued bombing and sanctioning of Iraq. The virulent criticism of America by the Taliban and bin Laden has resonated well in Pakistan.

More important than the lack of immediate public support for co-operating with the United States was concern about the reaction of the religious parties. Musharraf knew that they would quickly and vociferously take to the streets to vent their opposition to a positive response to the Americans. Although the President was reasonably sure that the security forces could contain trouble in the short run, he had to be concerned about what might happen were the U.S. military intervention in Afghanistan to become particularly bloody and protracted. If the fundamentalists succeeded eventually in staging massive anti-American and anti-government demonstrations in major cities throughout the country, especially in the Punjab, Musharraf's position would be in danger. . . .

Musharraf justified his positive response to the United States in a national television address on September 19, 2001. He first spelled out what help the United States had requested, but indicated that he did not know what U.S. plans were. Stressing that the decision was difficult, he argued that cooperating with the Americans was in Pakistan's interest, while refusing to do so presented grave dangers to the country. Refusal to cooperate, he declared, could even threaten Pakistan's sovereignty, its economy, its security assets (nuclear weapons) and its Kashmir policy. Making clear that he had India in mind, he undiplomatically told New Delhi to lay off.

Predictably, the religious parties took to the streets to oppose the decision after mid-day prayers two days later on September 21, 2001. The demonstrations were boisterous but largely limited to Peshawar and Quetta, where Afghani and Pakistani Pashtuns form the majority of the population, and to Pashtun areas of Karachi. The police contained the disorders and the rest of the country remained relatively quiet. Although public opinion opposed Musharraf's decision, he received the backing of the Muslim League and the Pakistan People's Party, the major mainstream political parties. They provided that backing partly because of the sheer horror of the terror attacks, and because about 250 Pakistanis or Pakistani-Americans died in the World Trade towers. The blindly negative stance of the Taliban in stonewalling last-minute Pakistani efforts to convince them to hand over bin Laden may also have been a factor.

Since Musharraf's initial decisions, Pakistani authorities have exerted more vigorous pressure on the religious groups than they have in the past. Maulana Fazlur Rehman, the firebrand leader of the Jamiat-e-Ulema Islam, the party closest to the Taliban, is under house arrest. The fact that Washington wisely decided to limit the use of Pakistan as a base of operations has also reduced the potential for political upheaval. In so doing, the Bush Administration showed sensitivity to Pakistani public opinion as well as to Pakistan's ambiguous position *vis-à-vis* the Taliban.

The rigidly inflexible attitude of the Taliban, which virtually invited the U.S. military response, has also enabled Musharraf to shift

Pakistani policy from trying to preserve the Taliban to writing them off. In reversing gears, Musharraf, in effect, has accepted that Pakistan's efforts to manipulate Afghanistan for its own purposes has reached a dead end. His focus has shifted to ensuring that a post-Taliban government is willing to accommodate more modest Pakistani interests—giving the Pashtuns a major voice and not adopting an anti-Pakistani policy. After years of the ISI's opposing any role for the exiled former King Zahir, Pakistan now speaks of him as an important transitional figure in shaping a post-Taliban Afghanistan. As events unroll in Afghanistan, Washington should not grant Pakistan a veto over U.S. policy toward Afghanistan, but it must recognize that no government in Kabul is likely to succeed for very long in the face of Pakistani opposition.

America's Interests

Once the dust settles in Afghanistan and a broad-based regime replaces the Taliban, it is essential that the United States not walk away as it did after the end of the Soviet war. A sustained international effort, preferably led by the United Nations, is needed to reconstruct Afghanistan after twenty years of devastation and disorder. As long as its legitimate interests in Afghanistan are taken into account, Pakistan has much to gain from such an outcome. A stable Afghanistan would permit the return of legitimate commerce, the opening up of new trade routes to Central Asia, the repatriation of Afghan refugees and far greater regional stability over all.

Domestically, too, U.S. interests will prosper if Musharraf successfully faces down the fundamentalists. By supporting Washington, Musharraf has crossed a Rubicon in opposing Pakistan's own extremists. If Pakistan can contain and reverse the pulse of Islamic radicalism, it will achieve greater internal stability than it has seen in many years. Increased aid inflows should have a positive impact on the Pakistani economy and permit the government to address some of Pakistan's basic economic shortcomings more seriously. Moreover, Musharraf held elections in October 2002 that indicate he might be committed to re-establishing a popularly elected government. Were he to veer from that commitment, the United States should make clear its displeasure. The system that emerges may not be Westminster democracy but it could offer what Pakistan badly needs—a period of political stability in a relatively free atmosphere.

The crystal ball is less clear with regard to India. The logic of the war against terrorism is clearly inconsistent with a continuation of active Pakistani support for *jihad* in Kashmir. It is hard to see how the United States can fight terrorism in Afghanistan while ignoring it in Kashmir. Nonetheless, the Kashmir struggle has become such an article of faith for the Pakistani military and much of the public that it will be politically difficult to shift gears. Washington should oppose *jihadi* operations in Kashmir more forcefully than it has in the past, but it should also press India to reduce its military presence and accept a more open political system inside the state.

Over the years, U.S.-Pakistan relations have been extraordinarily volatile. After a decade of difficulties, however, President Musharraf's response to the terrorist attacks of September 11 has reopened the possibility of a friendlier and more cooperative U.S.-Pakistan relationship. In moving forward, Washington needs to be clear-headed about where U.S. and Pakistani interests coincide, and where they do not. Too often in the past, both countries have overlooked underlying differences in the interest of attaining short-term goals. Washington should focus its assistance primarily on helping Pakistan to reform its economy to better provide for basic human needs. The United States should be wary, however, of again rewarding the generals with expensive and sophisticated military hardware. Quite apart from the damaging impact on U.S.-India relations such aid might cause, providing the 2002 equivalent of F-16s would serve neither U.S. nor Pakistani interests.

In the 1960s and the 1980s Pakistan stood on the edge of middle-income status, but failed to cross the threshold because of poor policy choices and unfortunate leadership. The outlook could improve were Pakistan to enjoy a period of political stability and sounder economic policies, and were it to focus its attention on addressing domestic ills rather than pursuing foreign adventures in Afghanistan and Kashmir. Pakistan could reverse its long downward slide, reduce the danger of religious extremism and make progress toward realizing its considerable potential as a middle power. There is a silver lining for Pakistan in the wake of the tragic events of September 11; it will take much work, however, to actually acquire the silver.

Pakistan Must Promote Democracy and Break Its Links with Militant Islamic Groups

By Benazir Bhutto

Benazir Bhutto is the oldest daughter of former Pakistani prime minister Zulfikar Ali Bhutto, who was ousted in a military coup in 1977 and executed in 1979. Ms. Bhutto, exiled for ten years, returned to Pakistan in 1986 to resume her leadership of the Pakistan People's Party—one of the largest mainstream political parties in Pakistan—and became the first female prime minister of a Muslim country in 1988. After being ousted on charges of corruption in 1990, she returned to power in 1993 only to be removed again in 1996 on similar charges. In the following selection, Bhutto claims that democratic reform is the best way to break the military's links to Islamic fundamentalists and to ensure a stable and peaceful future for Pakistan. Bhutto also argues that groups committed to democratic politics were responsible for keeping Islamic fundamentalism in check after Pervez Musharraf decided that Pakistan would support the American-led War on Terror.

The unspeakable sequence of terrorism in New York, Pennsylvania, and Washington, DC, on September 11, 2001, was a crime against humanity that sent a wave of revulsion throughout the civilized world—a world that will never be the same again. The lives of

Benazir Bhutto, "Pakistan's Dilemma: Breaking Links with the Past," *Harvard International Review*, Spring 2002, pp. 14–19. Copyright © 2002 by *Harvard International Review*. Reproduced by permission.

many people and many nations are now on the threshold of change. Pakistan's entrance into the international coalition against terror mirrored a broader worldwide development. Forces unleashed by the events of September 11 leave nations no choice when it comes to choosing where they stand. US President George Bush put it succinctly when he said, "Either you are with us or you are against us." Pakistan's cooperation re-invigorated its long-standing interaction with the United States, but the relationship will have moments of strain in these new circumstances. The dilemma that Pakistan now faces is that while it stands on the side of the forces aligned against international terror, it finds old linkages difficult to leave behind.

Breaking Links with the Taliban

The first repercussion of September 11 was the end of the Taliban regime that harbored Al Qaeda, but the engine of change in Kabul was the Northern Alliance's General Dostum rather than the Pakistani president, General Pervez Musharraf. The inability of Pakistan to engineer change in its own backyard where it previously enjoyed influence is significant. The military establishment has long viewed the Muslim Brotherhood as an ally because of its close alliance with the Pakistani military and security apparatus during the Cold War and its prevention of domestic socialist revolt. But the external forces unleashed by September 11 are forcing new political alignments that have led Pakistan to abandon some of its cherished policy goals. The first welcome casualty of the new Pakistani-US relationship was the long-standing romance between Pakistan's security apparatus and the rigid, extremist Taliban leadership. Yet the first tension in relations between the United States and Pakistan comes from their diverging viewpoints on the new Afghan interim government led by Hamid Karzai. Although Pakistan welcomed the Karzai government, it is uncomfortable with the leading role of the Northern Alliance.

The Pakistani military regime joined the US-led coalition against terror less from conviction than compulsion. Soon after September 11, President Musharraf appeared on state television to explain that he chose "the lesser evil" by joining the coalition and justified the move by saying that failure to do so could have damaged the country's nuclear assets. The notion of "compulsion" explains the inability of Pakistan to engineer the downfall of the Taliban or even to quickly break relations with it after the rout began. The long-term ties with the Taliban make Pakistan wary of the new internationally supported Afghan government. The ruling elites in Pakistan will seek an opportunity to re-assert their influence in Kabul by continuing linkages with some of the most extreme factions of the former *mu-*

jahideen, the freedom fighters that forced the Soviet Union out of Afghanistan.

Pakistan formulated its policy toward Afghanistan on the basis of "strategic depth." It saw in a pliable Afghan regime a foil to its uneasy relations with India, a country against which it has fought three wars since gaining its independence. Pakistan fears that its policy of strategic depth in Kabul will collapse if it discontinues support for the extremist factions. The Pakistani government does not believe that a friendly Afghan government is a sufficient guarantee of a secure border. The support for the Taliban produced linkages between the military and religious and militant groups. The ruling elites are finding it difficult to absorb the changes required of Pakistan as domestic linkages mesh with external requirements.

The second factor that causes concern in Pakistan is that breaking the linkages between the military, security apparatus, and religious groups could undermine its political support for the people of Jammu and Kashmir. The cornerstone of Pakistan's foreign policy is the dispute with India over control of this territory, leading both countries to seek weapons of mass destruction. While the United States may expect its ally to move against domestic groups related to Al Qaeda, Pakistan may find such a move impossible due to its own Kashmir policy. Ironically, even as the military regime joined the international coalition against terror, the groups closest to the Pakistani government took to the streets. The leaders of the religious parties with ties to militant groups held small, violent demonstrations, and some were put under house arrest. Those who remained free printed posters to recruit Pakistanis to fight the "holy war" on the side of the Taliban. They gathered young men who crossed into Afghanistan to fight in defense of Al Qaeda.

The principal reason General Musharraf's military regime was not overthrown by hard-liners in the military was the role played by the democratic forces in Pakistan. While the religious establishment's supporters took to the streets, their democratic opponents lent public support to the Musharraf government in its decision to join the international coalition. Surprisingly, the regime still treated the democratic forces harshly, keeping their popular leaders exiled.

The break with the constituency that backed the extremist Taliban has yet to come, and, unless it does, strains will persist in the Pakistani-US relationship. There are few signs so far that the present military regime plans to break links with the military, intelligence, political-religious, and militant groups. During the Cold War, the United States often supported dictators as the lesser evil in the war against communism. Now the United States is confronted with Pakistan as a military ally that it wishes to reward but that does not share its commitment to democratic values. Pakistan borders both Iran and Afghanistan—homes to two of recent history's Islamic revolutions. In Iran, it was the Ayatollah-driven Shia, and in Afghanistan it was the extreme Sunni movement that brought Mullah Omar [the leader of the Taliban] to power. The forces unleashed by these events left their own impact on Pakistan.

The Democratic Alternative

Too often the people of undemocratic countries find a democratic alternative lacking. Squeezed between the Western-backed dictator and the promise of change from the cleric-backed aspiring dictator, they turn to the clerics. For Pakistan's stability, it is important that the third choice of democracy be available.

Democracy is an issue of fundamental human rights, and the denial of the democratic aspirations of a people leads to the suppression of such movements. Silence is often sought through the cover of fabricated criminal charges, and the judicial system collapses as advocates of democracy are subjected to special laws and courts to uphold fabricated charges that violate due process. Undemocratic regimes also tend to enforce discrimination against women and minorities. The cumulative action against political dissidents, women, minorities, and other weak social groups strains the social fabric. Given the importance of human rights in the world today, the issue of democracy is one that will command attention in the dynamics of Pakistani-US relations.

Continued instability in Pakistan could create ethnic strains similar to those that destabilized countries of the former Soviet Union. Pakistan is a multiethnic nation that already partially disintegrated due to its inability to retain its East Pakistani Bengal population, which seceded to become Bangladesh in 1971. Now the challenge comes from the Pashtun-speaking population living on the border with Afghanistan. The Taliban was largely a Pashtun movement, and most of the demonstrations in Pakistan remained confined to the Pashtun belt where militancy and nationalism are on the rise. Complicating the issue is the fact that Pakistan and Afghanistan have yet to reach an agreement delineating the border between the two countries.

Political concerns have long plagued the border issue, beginning with the Durand Line left behind by the British as the demarcation between the two countries. Attempts at agreements to recognize the Durand Line as the international border failed in 1977, 1985, and most recently in 1989. The 1989 negotiations collapsed because the military was averse to signing a border agreement with the Afghan government because it ran contrary to its policy of strategic depth and the idea of a borderless Islamic world.

The linkages between the military, intelligence, and religious parties drew them into the relationship with the *maddrassas*, or religious schools, of which there are two types. Traditional schools teach the children how to read Arabic and the Quran, while the militant ones, established by the security apparatus during the Soviet occupation of Afghanistan, teach intolerance and hatred. It is from the latter that extreme factions of the *mujahideen* emerged. During the 1990s, these institutes moderated their curriculum to stay afloat. However, in 1996, after the overthrow of the democratic government by edict, the institutes went back to their old teachings, and their graduates formed new groups and private armed militias.

In light of its new relationship with the United States, Pakistan will face pressure to crack down on the militant teachings in the *maddrassas*, but this may be difficult. Ultimately, the power of the private militias, the militant *maddrassas*, and the political-religious parties depends on the support they receive from the military-security apparatus. Thus, reform becomes a key area in determining the success of Pakistan's new relationship with the West. The next few months could prove to be a crucial time for the armed forces of Pakistan to redirect their goals.

The direction of the Pakistani armed forces changed under the military rule of General Zia ul Haq, a protégé of the Muslim Brotherhood. For his own survival, Zia, at odds with the democratic forces, created an anti-democratic class of officers by resorting to the policies of the Muslim Brotherhood. The Afghan holy war against Soviet occupation enabled him to develop the concept of the holy role of the armed forces, which translated into guarding Pakistan's ideological frontiers in addition to its geographical borders. This change from a nationalistic army to a politically motivated one contributed to the domestic turmoil that Pakistan witnessed throughout the 1990s. Although Musharraf has taken steps to demote a few hard-line generals, he must still break links with the old establishment. This could prove difficult because of the close personal, social, and ideological bonds with Zia's theocratic worldview that Musharraf and other officers share. The officers may lack theocratic discipline in their personal behavior, but they remain committed to its political parameters. . . .

From Religion to the Gun

Pakistan's 20th-century alliance with the United States lasted the entire second half of the century but generated bitterness. As a loyal ally, Pakistan expected unconditional support from the United States, and resentment grew when Washington insisted on treating India and Pakistan equally during the 1965 Indo-Pakistani war. In 1971, this wound deepened. During the Bengali secessionist movement, Pakistan expected the United States to intercede on its behalf in Bangladesh. The United States did finally send its Seventh Fleet, and without this action the rest of Pakistan could have fallen as well. However, few Pakistanis were willing to rely on the United States after its flaccid support in Bangladesh.

The disintegration of Pakistan profoundly affected the leadership of the armed forces. Unable to accept culpability for the military defeat in Dacca, they blamed the defeat on United States and Pakistani politicians. The genocide that triggered Bangladesh's secession was buried as a dark secret, and three decades later, those responsible remain unapologetic and have never been tried.

During the anti-US Iranian revolution and the Soviet occupation of Afghanistan, Pakistan's position was strategic, and its military dictator was courted by all parties. General Zia ensured that ideology, dressed in religion, could be used to justify morally repugnant acts in the larger Islamic interest. He created a constituency based on a religiously motivated ideological movement through infiltration of the security apparatus, the army, the political parties, the judiciary, and the civil administration. The professional nature of the armed forces was abandoned in favor of political objectives.

The Soviet invasion of Afghanistan in 1979 opened a bonanza for Pakistan as billions of US dollars in military and economic assistance became available. For a ruler who allowed the Muslim Brotherhood to ride to Pakistan to burn the US embassy, this presented a dilemma. To justify support of the United States, Zia introduced the doctrine of necessity. He decided that the acceptance of arms and money to fight one superpower could be justified as part of a plan ultimately to fight another superpower.

The money for the fight against the Soviet occupation of Afghanistan was routed through the security apparatus, which set up educational institutes that trained extremist forces in Afghanistan and Pakistan. These institutes taught a form of Wahhabism, a school of religious interpretation similar to that of the powerful Saudi clergy, to which Pakistan's Muslim Brotherhood had close ties. Subsequently, during the Afghan *jihad*, when religious extremism was politically acceptable, networks were created among groups based in Pakistan to fight the Soviet infidels.

When Zia and his senior generals died in a 1988 plane crash, the mantle of leadership fell on Zia's close aides who were determined to turn Pakistan into a theocracy. The defining requirement for these officials was a Muslim ruler who would legislate as a spiritual leader, proscribing what is right and wrong in Islam. They placed their hopes on Zia's political heir, Chief Minister Nawaz Sharif. With their backing, Sharif twice formed a government and introduced legislation to turn Pakistan into a theocracy, but democratic opposition in parliament successfully blocked the legislation.

The return of democracy following Zia's death disappointed his generals. They felt that they and Zia had been used by the United States, which had turned a blind eye to dictatorship during the Soviet occupation. They re-established their identity and power by focusing on defeating another superpower, the United States, and the international atmosphere played into their hands. With the collapse of the Soviet Union and the fall of the Berlin Wall, world attention shifted to Europe and the newly emerging democracies. The *mujahideen* and their families turned to the *maddrassas* to school and feed their children. Their camps remained full of refugees living in squalor, and the only power they could exercise was the power of the gun.

On the Front Line in the War on Terror

Pakistan's establishment believed that it had defeated one superpower and could defeat another. They placed great hopes in the fighting capacity of the *mujahideen* while failing to realize that the Afghan occupation was a proxy war between the Soviets and US forces. Now Pakistan is back in the familiar, onerous role of a frontline state. The language defending Pakistan's decision to join the international coalition against terror is troubling. The military rulers, defending their decision once again on the doctrine of necessity, sent a message that feeds the Muslim psyche of injustice. The lingering frustrations of the last Afghan War and earlier Indo-Pakistani wars are reinforced for yet another generation.

Few in the Muslim world support the politics of the extremists, and a majority understands the need for the United States to protect its citizens and ensure that such an attack does not occur again. Yet fears abound that this may be a war against more than terrorists, that they are falling victim to a larger Western, Judeo-Christian action against Muslim civilization. There is a rising crescendo in the Muslim world to define "terrorism" itself, and some fear that indigenous national movements could be branded "terrorist" and crushed.

The rights of the Palestinians, the Kashmiris, and the Chechens are at the heart of regional disputes. They claim they are victims of state terror, whereas the states concerned accuse them of terrorism. By a twist of history, in many cases those fighting for national rights are Muslims, and those opposing them are non-Muslims.

Confidence must be instilled that the conflict with the terrorists is not a war against Islam. The perception that Muslim states, including Afghanistan, Iran, Iraq, Syria, and others are to fall one by one during the current campaign feeds such fears. The Pakistani conflict between theocratic and democratic forces mirrors the conflict in the larger Muslim world. Harvard Professor Samuel Huntington wrote a book about the "clash of civilizations"—a clash that is being played out in the mountain caves and tunnels of Afghanistan. The fight against the Taliban and the terrorists marks an important turning point in the direction the world will take in the 21st century.

One billion Muslims stand at the crossroads today, and they must choose between the forces of the past and the forces of the future. Pakistan, home to 140 million people, is crucial in this choice. The Pakistani-US relationship in the 21st century will be one of the most important ties for the United States. Neighboring Afghanistan with its access to Central Asia, Iran with its access to the Gulf, and India with its access to East Asia, Pakistan has great strategic importance. Its nuclear capability and dispute with India ensure that it will remain high on the US security agenda.

As the smoke billowed from the burning World Trade Center, the common refrain heard across cities and continents was, "The world will never be the same again."

The shock and horror that marked the sight of the mighty airplanes flying into New York's tallest buildings are unassailable. The most befitting tribute that Pakistan can pay to those who died in the ball of fire is to work with the United States to build a world where such acts of terror will never horrify us again.

Pakistan's Education Reform Efforts Will Fail

By Sajid Varda

Pervez Musharraf's decision to support the American war effort in Afghanistan drew heavy criticism from Islamic scholars, but his policies that aimed to reform Pakistani society were equally, if not more, controversial. One of Musharraf's reform efforts attempted to curb the influence of madrasas, *or Islamic schools, on Pakistani schoolchildren by controlling the curriculum and the budgets of the schools. The reforms were nominally designed to reverse the rise of radical Islamic groups and terrorist organizations in the region, which many Western analysts attributed to the fundamentalist teachings Muslim children received in Pakistani* madrasas. *However, many critics of these policies saw them as American efforts to control Pakistan and corrupt Muslim children with Western values. In the selection below, Sajid Varda, a global correspondent for* Khilafah Magazine, *argues that the reforms to Pakistan's educational system are an American plot to remove the influence of Islam in Pakistan and that these efforts are doomed to failure because of the righteousness of the Islamic community.*

Since the destruction of the Khilafah [Islamic state] in 1924, the kuffar [nonbelievers] have incessantly employed countless strategies to ensure the suppression of Islam through its agents stationed in the Muslim lands, who in turn oppress the ummah [community of believers] through their implementation of kufr [un-Islamic] policies.

One of the many tactics currently being adopted to halt any Islamic revival in Pakistan is through the clamping down on the madaaris [*madrasas*]. The government of Pakistan is recorded to spend a ridiculous 2% of its gross national output on public education. Its schools lack teachers, books, electricity, running water and in some cases even roofs. The literacy rate is estimated at around 40%. Withholding education from the public with the intention of creating backwardness and low levels of thinking amongst the people has backfired on the government. This has inadvertently led to the rise of the madrassah as an alternative, inexpensive schooling environment, which has now become the subject of focus by the US who believe that this source of Islamic education poses a serious threat to the western way of thinking and its corrupt values.

The Brookings Institute, which declares itself as an "Independent analyst and critic, committed to publishing its findings for the information of the public", is largely funded by wealthy individuals, corporations and other interest groups and serves a primary function to influence government policy. Its most recent study on the madaaris in Pakistan outlined actions that the US must take to reduce the influence of Islam. A closer scrutiny of these suggestions will reveal some interesting facts.

The report mentions that "inducements" need to be offered to ensure the successful registration of the madaaris, as well as finding ways of making additional funding available to replace the external foreign funding currently being received from private sources. It recommends that out of the further $500 million that is planned in US aid to Pakistan, "dedicated programs supporting education reforms" should be put in place.

A further tactic by the US is to provide food aid to schools via NGOs [Non-Governmental Organizations] to, "lure" students into the mainstream schools. There is the suggested bribery of madaaris leaders and teachers to teach within this "more controlled environment", however they make an important point that the US "should do nothing to implicate direct American government influence over them and thus discredit their Muslim credentials."

The US sponsorship of technical schools and centres of learning within Pakistan is also advocated. This vocational program can be achieved with the help of local and foreign companies (who would benefit from tax breaks and concessions) as well as through "small enterprise development programs run by aid agencies and NGOs."

Internship programs created in "moderate schools" would increase their attractiveness, as their students would be more successful at finding jobs. This measure is hoped will be appealing to willing madaaris. Finally, the report recommends highly that the US presence must be increased. This can be achieved by sending in local language speakers to take up important roles, i.e., in teaching, creating cultural centres and promoting educational exchanges involving the "paying of

American Islamic scholars" to speak within the many regions. These measures bear remarkable similarities to the ones adopted by the kuffar during the Uthmani Khilafah.

The US holds a grave fear of the rise of Islam and is exploring many avenues in achieving its aims.

The desire to follow such policies has been clearly shown in the most recent speech made by the ventriloquist's dummy, President Musharraf in January 2002. His hatred for Islam and loyalty to the contemporary Firawn [United States] was evident when he made the following statements:

"We have developed a new syllabi for them (madaaris) providing for the teaching of Pakistan studies, students of religious schools should be brought into the mainstream of society, this is the crux of the madrassa strategy. All madaaris will be registered by 23rd of March 2002 and no new madaaris will be opened without permission from the government."

It was not just the madaaris that were targeted; Musharraf went on to add:

"All mosques will be registered and no new mosques will be built without permission. The use of loudspeakers will be limited only to call for prayers, and Friday Sermon."

"People who do not mix religion with politics are blessed with wisdom and vision," he said.

This last comment truly illustrates the US fear of political Islam.

In response to Musharraf's speech, the US Secretary of State Colin Powell stated: "I welcome President Musharraf's speech. He has taken a bold and principled stand to set Pakistan squarely against terrorism and extremism both in and outside of Pakistan. The United States applauds the banning of Jaish-e-Mohammad and Lashkar-e-Tayyiba and welcomes President Musharraf's explicit statements against terrorism and particularly notes his pledge that Pakistan will not tolerate terrorism under any pretext, including Kashmir."

The real US Ambassador to Pakistan, Pervez Musharraf, has connived and planned with the White House to further secularise Islam in Pakistan. The long running debate over controlling the educational curriculum especially within madaaris has again become the focus of Musharraf's government. The accusation against these estimated 45,000 schools is that they teach a disliking of the west and seek to propagate Islam through jihad.

It is only through the above measures that the US via Musharraf can sustain and build the secular education system in Pakistan, with the specific aim of creating a future generation of Muslims detached from Islam and moulded by the US to give up jihad and the struggle to make the word of Allah the highest.

The US and the likes of Musharraf need to understand that their desire to destroy Islam and ensure its system is never implemented will amount to nothing, as Allah says:

"They wish to extinguish Allah's Light with their mouths, but Allah will not allow but that His Light is perfected even though the Kuffar may detest it" [The Holy Quran At-Tauba: 32].

The Islamic ummah must realise that its comprehensive revival will only occur through the reestablishment of the Khilafah and the implementation of the Islamic education system based upon the Islamic aqeedah [system of belief], covering all aspects of science, technology, mathematics, politics and spirituality. This will ensure the domination of the Islamic thoughts and the rejection of corrupt western influences and ideas.

Pakistan Needs a Strong Leader

By David Pryce-Jones

David Pryce-Jones studied history at Magdalen College in Oxford, England, and is currently the senior editor of the National Review, *a conservative newsmagazine. He has followed political and social developments in the Arab world for many years and has published numerous books and articles, including* A Closed Circle: An Interpretation of the Arabs. *In this essay, Pryce-Jones compares Pakistan's Pervez Musharraf to the founder of modern Turkey, Mustafa Kemal, or Ataturk. The author argues that strong, dictatorial leadership from the general-president in the short term is the best way to solve the problems of religious fundamentalism and sectarian violence in Pakistan. Eliminating the culture of violence would not only put Pakistan on a path toward stable democracy, but it would also be a crucial step toward eliminating international terrorism.*

G en. Pervez Musharraf is every inch a professional soldier. On October 12, 1999, he was army chief of staff in Pakistan and flying home from a visit to Sri Lanka. He had recently fired a senior officer for meeting the Pakistani prime minister Nawaz Sharif without permission. Musharraf was pleased with himself; but Sharif felt insulted. A power struggle was underway.

Calculating that Musharraf couldn't do much about it in mid-air, Sharif fired him. Wrong. Landing at Karachi airport, Musharraf arranged a coup, put Sharif on trial, and sent him into exile in Saudi Arabia. Musharraf installed himself in Sharif's place. That's the way politics are conducted pretty much throughout the Muslim world. Personalities in this context are real, while principles are nebulous.

The military is the one and only institution in Pakistan that can be said to function. It is unwise to tamper with it. Military coups occur at regular intervals, and the country has had long spells under mar-

David Pryce-Jones, "Ataturk II?" *National Review*, vol. 54, February 25, 2002, pp. 32–34. Copyright © 2002 by National Review, Inc. Reproduced by permission.

tial law—without which it would have disintegrated into anarchy. An assortment of different peoples and languages are engaged in permanent jostling, without benefit of democracy or the rule of law. Government writ does not hold in the northwest frontier where al-Qaeda and maybe Osama bin Laden could be sheltering. In major cities like Lahore and Karachi, people die regularly in obscure shootings, whether committed by political extremists or criminals. Civil society does not exist. What has brought these people together is only the chance that they are all Muslims.

In the words of a famous clerihew, that peculiar but pointed verse form, "George the Third / Ought never to have occurred. / One can only wonder / At so grotesque a blunder." Pakistan ought never to have occurred either, and one can only wonder at the way the British manufactured it without regard to what they themselves believed, and ignoring the experience of two centuries of empire.

Governing the Indian subcontinent, the British were careful to keep the balance between Hindus and Muslims. Although predisposed by temperament to favor the Muslims—who seemed to them livelier and more capable than the Hindus—they administered the law impartially, and laid the basis for the democracy that India itself is now perpetuating. Responsible Muslim leaders were on equal terms with their Hindu counterparts, and Muslim extremism appeared to be a thing of the past.

At the start of the 20th century, the British honored a promise to initiate a public debate about the coming of self-rule for the peoples of the empire. In a reaction that surprised them, this provoked an identity crisis everywhere. From India to Egypt to Ireland, the resulting wave of nationalism is still working itself out. Hindus had their National Congress, and Muslims should have been encouraged to join it in a power-sharing spirit. Instead, one of the viceroy's advisers, a man with the resonant name of William Shakespear, suggested that Muslims should form a counterpart, known as the Muslim League.

Out of such seeds were to grow the division of the subcontinent into two religious and national communities contending for supremacy in fear of each other; then three countries (with Bangladesh splitting away from Pakistan—probably one day there will be a fourth country, Kashmir); and so incessant warfare; and now finally a nuclear standoff. In 1947, the British agreed to partition and immediately scuttled home ashamed of themselves, to allow all on the ground to do their worst and finalize the horrors to come. Millions of people were left at one another's throat.

Why independent India succeeded while independent Pakistan

failed is a question inviting many answers, having to do with religion and culture, expectation, circumstances, bad government, and various imponderables. In one of his penetrating phrases, V.S. Naipaul has written that to most Muslims the state that had been won out of the subcontinent came "as a kind of religious ecstasy, something beyond reason, beyond quibbles about borders and constitutions." Nothing to do with democracy, the Muslim League and other political parties have been so many religious or ethnic mass movements whereby ambitious individuals lever themselves into absolute power.

Islamic Militancy in Pakistan

The ruling elite has mercilessly exploited the religious ecstasy that came with the birth of the state. Pakistan today is second only to Saudi Arabia as a source of Islamic militancy. Islam provides an identity above ethnicity, tribe, or clan. Some 7,000 madrassahs, or religious seminaries, fanaticize otherwise uneducated boys by teaching them to memorize the Koran in Arabic (which is not their language, and which they do not understand), and no other subjects at all. Thousands of mullahs preach incendiary sermons in order to mobilize the mob against unbelievers. In the supposed cause of Islam, successive rulers have sponsored and exploited a variety of militant groups, notably the Taliban in Afghanistan, and Jaish-e-Muhammad and Lashkar-e-Taiba to terrorize Kashmir. The military and its most powerful agency, the Inter-Services Intelligence force, the ISI, exploited Islamic extremism by means of a doctrine of "strategic depth" whose purpose was to spread Pakistani influence in Kashmir and throughout Central Asia.

Reckless adventure of this sort has generated corruption and a foreign policy based on terror, carrying the recurrent risk of war with India and other neighbors. Every method, including assassination, has been used to silence intellectual opponents and dissidents, and to cow the population at large. An undeclared civil war rages between Islamic militants and secular-minded moderates. Equally caught up in its vision of religious ecstasy and equally indifferent to the fate of the masses, the ruling elite in Saudi Arabia has oil wealth at its disposal, while in Pakistan debt servicing already accounts for over half the budget. The country is on the edge of bankruptcy. Two emotional foreign policies fused when Saudi Arabia financed Pakistan to build the "Islamic nuclear bomb" that destabilizes the region far and wide.

Musharraf's coup was bloodless, and widely welcomed in long-suffering and lawless Pakistan. To brake the descent of his country into the abyss, he would need all the powers at his disposal, however arbitrary and undemocratic these might be. The Clinton administration's reaction, however, was to "seek the earliest possible restoration of democracy in Pakistan." The State Department spokesman said that "Pakistan's constitution must be respected, not only in the letter but in its spirit." This was fantasy, as though the Pakistani constitution were like the American. In Pakistan, the constitution is what the ruler, the army, and the ISI decide it is. The British were equally comical and ignorant in their response. Robin Cook, the foreign secretary at the time, deplored the coup, and Peter Hain, a reliably wrong-headed junior minister, gave the empty boast that "Britain will act very firmly to ensure Pakistan receives no international support and is penalized as strongly as possible diplomatically."

For Islamic militants in Pakistan, the events of September 11 signified that their hour of triumph had come. In a spasm of religious ecstasy, thousands rushed to join the Taliban and al-Qaeda, and many tens of thousands mobilized in the cities for demonstrations that were almost uprisings. Musharraf at once understood that he was between a rock and a hard place: He had to decide which side he was on in the undeclared civil war between Islamic extremists and secular moderates. This was nothing less than an existential choice over the future of Pakistan.

All other leaders in Muslim countries have confronted this same choice about the ultimate role of Islam and Islamic militants. They have made sure to assert full control by such means as setting up an official ministry responsible for the appointment of mullahs and preachers, and nationalizing religious property. Should skillful maneuvers of this kind fail, they have not hesitated to suppress and eliminate their Islamists with whatever violent means available, including massacres, judicial executions, and life sentences in prison. What they cannot tolerate is the threat posed to their dictatorship by Islamic extremists.

The Turkish Precedent

Mustapha Kemal, otherwise known as Ataturk, or "father of the Turks," set the first and most striking precedent. The Ottoman Empire had been the foremost Muslim power in the world until its defeat in the First War. The one and only successful Ottoman general in that war, Ataturk afterwards staged a bloodless coup to seize power for himself and to use it in order to constitute modern Turkey out of the wreckage. Islam, in his view, was a total obstacle to modernization and had to be reformed out of all recognition. Andrew Mango, his authoritative biographer, calls him a free thinker, and quotes him saying to a reporter, "I have no religion, and at times I wish all religions at the bottom of the sea. He is a weak ruler who needs religion to uphold his people. . . . My people are going to learn the principles of democracy, the dictates of truth, and the teachings of science. Superstition must go. Let them worship as they will; every man can follow his own conscience."

The aim was to disestablish Islam. A new Ministry of Religious Affairs allowed Ataturk to administer Islam and the mullahs for his purposes. Using strong-arm methods where necessary, he closed the madrassahs and suppressed the extremist orders of dervishes. He is said personally to have punched recalcitrant mullahs and to have ordered the destruction of a mosque that spoiled his view. His fondness for alcohol and womanizing was no secret. Traditional Islamic dress, including the veil for women, was outlawed. After he had finished, Islam was no longer the official state religion, and the foundations of secularism were well and truly laid. Turkey has since changed its government through democratic election, as Ataturk intended. True, in recent times there have been military coups and interludes of martial law. True too, Islamic extremists have made a comeback, and even formed a government, and the secular parties have resorted to undemocratic stratagems to keep them out of politics. Even with these imperfections, Turkey today may claim to be the one and only Muslim country with any democratic credentials.

Musharraf is now in the Ataturk position, a dictator deploying absolute power for the apparently paradoxical ends of modernizing and democratizing. Like Ataturk, he has to work in chaotic conditions to create a nation-state capable of dealing with the difficulties it faces. He made his existential choice when he broke with the Taliban, joined the American coalition, and opened local air bases to American aircraft. He has also purged senior generals in the army and the ISI who were Islamists and promoters of the "strategic depth" doctrine that has wreaked such havoc. He has banned Jaish-e-Muhammad and Lashkar-e-Taiba and several other terror groups as well, closing 500 of their offices and ordering the tracking of their funds with the aim of freezing them. In the most fraught part of this U-turn, he has had arrested an estimated 2,000 militants who until now were secretly subsidized and encouraged by the ISI. He describes madrassahs correctly as places that "propagate hatred and violence," and in the future they will have to register with the authorities and teach modern courses. Rival politicians and influential opinion-makers who hitherto have criticized Musharraf for usurping democratic rule are now coming around to him because Pakistan has changed course and will not become an extremist Islamist state. Democracy, he told the nation in a televised broadcast, is the long-term objective.

Islam and democracy, as Ataturk discovered, prove to be incompatible ideals. Musharraf looks set to become the second dictator to break political and militant Islam for the sake of democracy. This requires personal courage, and the successful outcome of the American war on terror. Democratizing Pakistan, he would also be in a position to abate the grotesque blunder of partitioning British India on religious lines. It is a tall order, but he has a chance to go down in history as a great man.

The West Will Abandon Pakistan

By Andrew Roberts

Andrew Roberts is a writer and historian, and is currently an honorary se-nior scholar at Gonville and Caius College in Cambridge, England. In the following excerpt, Roberts argues that Western nations have demonstrated a tendency to abandon their Third World allies when they outlive their useful-ness—a tendency that he believes will one day manifest itself in South Asia. Roberts argues that the United States and Britain will also neglect Pakistan's needs once the war in Afghanistan ends. Accordingly, he maintains that Pak-istani president Pervez Musharraf unintentionally laid the foundation for his future demise when he agreed to support the War on Terror.

In serving the West, no good deed goes unpunished, for as the old Arab adage goes, 'Oppose the West and they'll buy you off; sup-port it and they'll sell you off.' In the past America has protected her local strongmen, but today, as Pakistan's General Pervez Musharraf contemplates his long-term career prospects, modern history provides all too many examples to show that he will not last long once his use-fulness to the West is over.

During the Truman, Eisenhower, Kennedy, Nixon and Ford ad-ministrations, America tended to stand by her clients in the Third World, not displaying inquisitiveness into their domestic political arrangements so long as they delivered regional stability and pursued a doughty anti-communist agenda. Yet since the decline of Kissin-gerian realpolitik and its replacement by utopian liberal internation-alism—particularly during the Carter and Clinton presidencies—there has been a long and sorry history of the United States letting down her clients, both in public and private, over small issues and large ones. Defending Western interests in the developing world has thus become a completely thankless task.

The Fickle West

Although General Musharraf is now being feted by Washington, fawned on by Colin Powell, offered vast sums in debt relief by the US Treasury and boosted by a Britain that only six months ago wished to kick him out of the Commonwealth, he does not need to look too far either geographically or historically to see how fickle are the West's affections. Recent history is littered with the fates of regional strongmen who have been cast aside—or worse—the moment they have served their purpose.

Mohammad Reza Pahlavi was crowned Shah of Persia in 1941, and kept his country resolutely pro-Western, capitalist, anti-fundamentalist and anti-communist until he was overthrown by Ayatollah Khomeini in January 1979. As is documented in William Shawcross's masterly *The Shah's Last Ride*, Washington then dropped him completely, and he died aged 60 in Cairo in July 1980, having been refused access to the best American healthcare.

Doing America's dirty work for her in Central America at much the same time was Anastasio Somoza, who in July 1979 was forced to flee Nicaragua, where he and his father had been fighting communism for decades. He died in Asuncion, Paraguay, the following year after he, too, had been denied the right to reside in the United States. At least Ferdinand Marcos, the strongman who held the Philippines against communist insurgency for 20 years, was not banned from entering America after the US dumped him in 1986; he was allowed to go into exile in Honolulu, where he died three years later. . . .

Probably the most shameful betrayal of any friend of the West was committed by the Blair ministry between 1998 and 2000 when General Augusto Pinochet, who had saved Chile from communism and civil war in 1973 and voluntarily relinquished power in March 1990, was kept under house arrest here for a whole year pending possible extradition. The White House, which could and should have done much to make the Blair administration see sense over this dreadful episode, did nothing. Gratitude for past services is forgotten in post-Kissingerian Western foreign policy, yet if the War on Terror is to be won, it had better be relearned.

Bleak Prospects

It is not difficult to predict that even if he survives fundamentalist resolutions and al-Qa'eda suicide bombers, General Musharraf will one day be brought down by precisely those Western countries that are now his most ardent suitors. He is in far more danger trusting us than ever he was when operating behind enemy lines . . . during the India-Pakistan wars.

Imagine if either of Pakistan's recent former prime ministers, Nawaz Sharif or Benazir Bhutto—people whose careers were based on corruption and compromise—had been in charge in Islamabad rather than the rock-like war hero Musharraf. The story of Pakistan's support for the War on Terror would undoubtedly have been very different, and very much worse for us. Yet the prospects for the greatest man in the subcontinent, once the War on Terror has been won, look bleak. On past performance, the best that the West can offer her new best friend is the choice between exile, a jail sentence, multiple visa refusals, a year-long house arrest, an early grave, or a lonely struggle in the African jungle with no end in sight. Hardly a tempting prospect for those whose support we might want in any future conflicts. At present, we are feting General Musharraf, but it is in the nature of our feckless, ungrateful, modern foreign policy that one day we will bury him.

♦ IMPORTANT FIGURES

Sheikh Muhammad Abdullah (1905–1982) A Kashmiri nationalist the British government frequently imprisoned for his work in the Indian independence movement. After India and Pakistan gained their independence from Britain in 1947, Abdullah became the prime minister of Kashmir, but he was removed from his position in 1953 after he criticized the Indian government for its treatment of Muslims on the Indian side of the 1948 cease-fire line.

Sir Sayyid Ahmad Khan (1817–1898) A nineteenth-century Muslim intellectual and the founder of Aligarh College (1877) near Delhi. Ahmad Khan's college produced many of the leading Muslim separatists that successfully pressed for the establishment of a Muslim state in South Asia.

Mohammad Ayub Khan (1907–1974) Former commander in chief of the Pakistani armed forces who became president of Pakistan (1958–1969) through a military coup. Ayub Khan engineered Pakistan's second constitution and orchestrated its involvement in the 1965 war with India.

Benazir Bhutto (1953–) The daughter of Zulfikar Ali Bhutto and two-time prime minister of Pakistan (1988–1990; 1993–1996). She was the first woman to become the political leader of a Muslim country, but was twice ousted on charges of corruption and mismanagement by her political opponents.

Zulfikar Ali Bhutto (1928–1979) The founder of the Pakistan People's Party (PPP), deputy prime minister during the presidency of Yahya Khan, and the prime minister of Pakistan (1973–1977) until he was ousted in a military coup. Bhutto was an important contributor to the third Pakistani constitution (1973) and was the first prime minister to authorize the military and tactical support of Islamic groups in Afghanistan.

Mohandas Karamchand Gandhi (1869–1948) The former president of the Indian National Congress (1924) and leader of the noncooperation movement of 1920, the civil disobedience campaign of 1928, and the Quit India movement of 1942. Although Gandhi was a Hindu and an Indian nationalist, his efforts contributed to the independence of both India and Pakistan from Great Britain.

Mohammad Iqbal (1877–1938) An Urdu "poet philosopher" and former president of the All-India Muslim League (1930). Iqbal was among the first to press for separate Muslim states in British India. Though he did not advocate complete independence, his ideas were very influential on the Muslim League and served as the intellectual foundation for the Pakistan movement.

Ghulam Ishaq Khan (1915–) The former president of the Senate that became president of Pakistan (1988–1993) after the death of Zia-ul-Haq in 1988. Ishaq Khan oversaw the elections of 1988 that temporarily restored democratic politics to Pakistan. The period of Ishaq Khan's presidency was marred by political infighting and turmoil that prompted the army to dismiss him in 1993.

Mohammed Ali Jinnah (1876–1948) The president of the All-India Muslim League (1934–1947) and the first governor general of Pakistan (1947–1948). Many historians argue that without Jinnah, the Muslim League would not have successfully campaigned for a separate Muslim state in South Asia.

Mohammed Khan Junejo (1932–1992) The handpicked prime minister (1985–1988) of General Zia-ul-Haq. Junejo oversaw the restoration of party politics in Pakistan after a long period of one-party, military rule, but he was removed by Zia once he directly challenged the general's authority in military affairs.

Farooq Ahmad Khan Leghari (1940–) A loyal member of Zulfikar Ali Bhutto's Pakistan People's Party that became president of Pakistan (1993–1997) during Benazir Bhutto's second administration. During a political crisis in 1996, Leghari dissolved the Pakistani Parliament and dismissed Ms. Bhutto on charges of corruption, opening the door for Mian Nawaz Sharif to become prime minister for the second time in five years.

Liaquat Ali Khan (1895–1951) The first lieutenant of Mohammed Ali Jinnah and president of the All-India Muslim League (1948–1956) during the period between independence and the ratification of the first Pakistani constitution. Liaquat Ali Khan also served as the first prime minister of Pakistan.

Lord Louis Mountbatten (1900–1979) The last viceroy of British India (1946–1947). Mountbatten oversaw the independence process and the division of British India into separate Muslim and Hindu states.

Mujib-ur-Rahman (1922–1975) The former head of East Pakistan's (now Bangladesh) Awami League, a political party that pressed for more autonomy for the government of East Pakistan. Mujib was elected as East Pakistan's representative to the National Assembly in 1970 and might have been able to take over the prime minister's position, but General Yahya Khan rejected his program and attempted to arrest Mujib and some of his associates. These events ultimately led to the 1971 war with India and the secession of East Pakistan.

Pervez Musharraf (1943–) The president (1999–) and chief of army staff of Pakistan. Musharraf achieved power through a military coup in 1999 and became an important American ally in the War on Terror that began in the fall of 2001. His efforts to reform Pakistani politics were crucial for the American war effort and for improving relations with India.

Mian Nawaz Sharif (1949–) The two-time prime minister of Pakistan (1990–1993; 1997–1999) who was removed in a military coup in 1999. Nawaz Sharif was a political opponent of Benazir Bhutto and became prime minister after she was removed in 1990 and in 1997 because of his popularity in the Punjab and his acceptability to military leaders.

Akhtar Abdur Rahman (1924–1988) The chairman of the joint chiefs of staff during Zia-ul-Haq's military regime. Rahman was also the director general of the Inter-Services Intelligence (1979–1987) and was responsible for the conduct of Pakistan's aid to the mujahideen against Soviet forces in Afghanistan. He was killed along with Zia-ul-Haq in a plane crash in 1988.

Agha Mohammed Yahya Khan (1917–1980) The former president of Pakistan (1969–1971) who assumed power through a military coup that replaced the administration of Ayub Khan. Yahya Khan presided over one of the most tumultuous periods in Pakistani history, which witnessed a bloody civil war in East Pakistan (now Bangladesh) and a war with India in Kashmir.

Mohammad Zia-ul-Haq (1924–1988) The former president of Pakistan (1978–1988). Zia-ul-Haq took power in a military coup that removed Zulfikar Ali Bhutto from power in 1977. He also launched an aggressive campaign to strengthen the influence of Islam in Pakistan—a program that included support for the Afghan mujahideen during the war against the Soviets—before he was killed in a plane crash in 1988.

🔥 GLOSSARY

Azad Kashmir: The Pakistani-controlled portion of the disputed region of Kashmir.

Bangladesh: A part of the state of Bengal in British India that became East Pakistan after the British granted independence to its South Asian empire in 1947. Pakistan fought a particularly bloody civil war in which the Bengalis of East Pakistan pressed for independence; they succeeded with the aid of India in December 1971. East Pakistan was renamed Bangladesh upon its independence.

Comprehensive Test Ban Treaty: An international treaty that was opened for signature on September 24, 1996. The goals of the treaty are to prevent the testing of nuclear weapons and to prevent the proliferation of nuclear weapons, especially by states that do not yet possess them. As of this writing, Pakistan and India have refused to ratify the treaty.

Deobandi movement (Deobandis): An Islamic political movement that began in the Indian city of Deoband in the mid–nineteenth century. Like the Wahabi movement in Saudi Arabia, the Deobandi movement seeks the removal of all non-Muslim influences from Islamic culture, including the use of Western science. Unlike the Wahabis, the Deobandis did not preach overt confrontation with other cultures.

Durand Line: The ill-defined border between Afghanistan and Pakistan. In 1793, the British reached an agreement with the Afghan king Abdul Rahman Khan to separate British India from Afghanistan at what became known as the Durand Line. When the British granted independence to Pakistan in 1947, Afghanistan disputed the legality of the border, which continues to be a source of conflict between Pakistan and Afghanistan.

Glenn Amendment: An amendment to the American Foreign Assistance Act of 1961. Passed by the U.S. Congress in 1977, the amendment prohibits American aid to any non–nuclear weapon state that tests a nuclear warhead. The United States first imposed Glenn Amendment sanctions on India and Pakistan in 1998.

Harkat-ul-Mujahideen: Formerly called Harkat-ul-Ansar, this group is the oldest of the three largest Islamic separatist groups that operate in Kashmir. Indian officials claim that Harkat-ul-Mujahideen, which means "movement of the holy warriors," is trained and armed by the Pakistani military and blame the group for the hijacking of an Indian Airlines jet in December 1999.

Hezb-ul-Mujahideen: The largest Islamic separatist group operating in Kashmir in the mid-1990s. Hezb-ul-Mujahideen developed with the support of the Pakistani government, which shared the organization's goal of Kashmiri accession to Pakistan. Because of ideological differences, especially its connections with the Pakistani political party Jamaat-i-Islami, Hezb-ul-Mujahideen distanced itself from the Pakistani government and began operating with a degree of independence in the late 1990s.

Inter-Services Intelligence (ISI): The Pakistani agency responsible for gathering foreign and domestic intelligence. The Inter-Services Intelligence worked closely with the American Central Intelligence Agency during the Soviet-Afghan War of 1979 to 1989 and continues to take an active role in the internal politics of Afghanistan and Kashmir by supporting militant Islamic groups.

Jaish-e-Muhammad: A militant Islamic separatist group that continues to fight for the overthrow of Indian forces in Kashmir. Jaish-e-Muhammad, or "the army of Muhammad," has been linked to several violent acts in India and Kashmir, including an attack on the Indian Parliament building in December 2001 that brought India and Pakistan to the brink of war.

Jamaat-e-Ulema-e-Islam: A Pakistani political party that advocates a theocratic state in Pakistan based on the tenets of Islam. Jamaat-e-Ulema-e-Islam, or "the party of Islamic scholars," is also an active supporter of Kashmiri militant groups, especially the Harkat-ul-Mujahideen.

Jamaat-i-Islami: A political party founded in 1941 by the Muslim cleric Maulana Sayyid Abul Ala Maududi. Jamaat-i-Islami, or "the Islamic party," pressed vehemently for the advent of an Islamic state in Pakistan and recently called for Muslims to overthrow the Pakistani government if it did not stop its support for the American War on Terror.

Jammu and Kashmir: The Indian-controlled portion of the disputed region of Kashmir.

jihad: An Arabic word commonly translated as "holy war." Jihad is an orthodox Islamic injunction for all Muslims to spread Islam by waging war against non-Muslim cultures. The duty of jihad does not necessarily include physical war; there are four ways in which a Muslim can fulfill his or her duty of jihad. The most common way is to wage war in one's own heart by resisting inducements to commit acts contrary to the Koran and the laws of Islam (Sharia).

Kargil: A city in Indian-controlled Kashmir that was the site of a small-scale Pakistani military offensive against India in May 1999.

Kashmir: A disputed territory straddling northwest India and northeast Pakistan. It is divided into two sections: Indian-controlled Jammu and Kashmir, and Pakistani-controlled Azad Kashmir.

Lashkar-e-Taiba: A militant Islamic separatist group in Kashmir that is based in Pakistan. Lashkar-e-Taiba, which means "army of the pure," conducted several violent operations against both civilian and military targets in Indian-controlled Kashmir, adding to tensions between India and Pakistan throughout the 1990s.

Line of Control (LoC): The border between Pakistani-controlled and Indian-controlled Kashmir that is the result of the terms that ended the Indo-Pakistani War of 1971.

madrasas: The Arabic word for "schools," or religious schools. Historically, teachers in the *madrasas* of South Asia instructed Muslim students on religious matters in addition to other subjects such as mathematics and astronomy. Since the Soviet-Afghan War of 1979 to 1989, *madrasas* have grown in number and are increasingly associated with the Wahabi movement, which teaches a strict form of Islam and in some cases advocates violence against non-Muslim cultures.

Moguls (Mughals): A Muslim dynasty in South Asia that began with the rule of the Turkish chieftain Babur (1483–1530) in 1526. The Moguls controlled much of modern-day India and Pakistan for three centuries and were one of the largest Asian empires until the British consolidated their control over India in 1857.

mujahideen: A word that translates from both Farsi and Arabic to mean "those who fight the holy war." The mujahideen were an alliance of several different Muslim groups based in Pakistan and Iran that fought against the Soviet Union in Afghanistan during the war of 1979 to 1989.

mullah: A title of honor reserved for Islamic religious scholars meaning "lord" or "master." There are no formal requirements for a Muslim to become a mullah, but usually those who receive the title graduate from a *madrasa,* or religious school, and are extremely well versed in the Koran or are prayer leaders in a mosque. The term also refers to those who are traditionally responsible for the interpretation of Islamic law (Sharia).

Northern Alliance: A group of non-Pashtun rebel groups that fought against the Taliban regime in Afghanistan from 1996 to 2002. While Pakistan backed the Taliban, the Northern Alliance received aid from India, Iran, and Russia.

Nuclear Nonproliferation Treaty: An international treaty signed by 187 countries in 1970. The treaty was designed to prevent the spread of nuclear weapons to non–nuclear weapons states and to encourage the five nuclear powers recognized in the treaty (Britain, China, France, the Soviet Union, and the United States) to disarm their nuclear warheads.

Pandits: A Hindu minority group in Kashmir. Pandits arrived in the Kashmir valley in approximately 3000 B.C. and continue to make a tremendous contribution to Kashmiri culture. Pandits lived in relative harmony with Muslims until the partition of British India in 1947; they have since been subjected to violence and persecution by militant Islamic separatists in Kashmir.

Pashtunistan: A term that refers to the goal of ethnic Pashtuns in Afghanistan and Pakistan to create a separate, or semiautonomous, state in the area that consists of territories in northwest Pakistan and eastern Afghanistan. The separatist pressure that the Pashtunistan movement exerted on Pakistani political leaders was one of the factors that led them to pursue the policy of strategic depth (the Pakistani support of Islamic militants in Afghanistan).

Pressler Amendment: An amendment to the American Foreign Assistance Act of 1961. Passed by the U.S. Congress in 1985, the amendment restricts the amount of economic and military aid the United States can give Pakistan unless the president of the United States verifies that Pakistan does not possess nuclear weapons or the aid reduces the risks associated with Pakistan's possessing a nuclear weapon.

Punjab: A region in northern India and eastern Pakistan in which the three largest religious groups—Hindus, Muslims, and Sikhs—are all very prominent. The British divided the Punjab between Pakistan and India in 1947, a decision that led to widespread religious violence between all three groups and to the first war between India and Pakistan in 1948.

al-Qaeda: A militant Islamic group formed in 1989 by Osama bin Laden and Muhammad Atef. Al-Qaeda, which means "the base" in Arabic, is devoted to removing the American military from Saudi Arabia and opposing non-Islamic governments around the world.

Sharia: The religious laws of Islam. Muslims are bound to act in all social and ritualistic functions according to the Sharia, which is based on four tenets: the Koran, the example of the prophet Muhammad, the consensus of Muslim scholars, and reasoning by analogy to existing laws when no precedent exists in the Koran or the teachings of the prophet Muhammad.

Shia Islam (Shiites): The second largest branch of Islam—making up 10 to 15 percent of all Muslims—which developed after the death of the prophet Muhammad in A.D. 632. The Shiites supported Muhammad's son-in-law, Ali, as the successor to the earthly political leadership of Muslims. The support of Ali as Muhammad's successor created a division between Shiites and the largest branch of Islam, the Sunnis.

Sikhs: The third major religious group in South Asia. The Guru Nanak founded the Sikh religion, which combines elements of Hinduism and Islam, in the fifteenth century. The majority of

Sikhs live in the Punjab, a state that was divided between Pakistan and India when the two countries gained their independence from Britain in 1947.

Sipah-e-Sahaba: A Sunni political organization that has been accused of terrorist violence against the Shiite minority in Pakistan. Sipah-e-Sahaba, or "army of the companions," was one of the most vocal opponents of Pervez Musharraf's decision to support the American-led War on Terror and was outlawed by presidential decree on January 12, 2002.

South Asian Association for Regional Cooperation (SAARC): A regional organization formed in 1985 that is nominally devoted to the cooperation and mutual benefit of South Asian countries. The member states of the SAARC are Bangladesh, Bhutan, India, Maldives, Nepal, Pakistan, and Sri Lanka.

strategic depth: A term that refers to Pakistan's foreign policy of supporting radical Islamic groups in Afghanistan during the 1970s through the 1990s. The Pakistanis pursued this policy in order to install a government in Afghanistan that would be sympathetic to Pakistan's interests and capable of supporting Pakistan in the event of a war with India.

Sunni Islam (Sunnis): The largest branch of Islam, approximately 85 to 90 percent of all Muslims. After the death of Muhammad in A.D. 632, the Sunni Muslims recognized the need to centralize political leadership in an institution called the caliphate. The political leader, or caliph, was chosen according to a consensus of Muslim political leaders rather than on the principle of spiritual purity as advocated by the Shiites.

Wahabi movement (Wahabis): A political movement that emerged in present-day Saudi Arabia in the mid–eighteenth century. Established by Ibn 'Abd al-Wahhab, the Wahabis emerged to eradicate all nonorthodox groups and influences they perceived as threats to Islamic tradition. The Wahabi School advocates a strict interpretation of Islamic law (Sharia) and continues to influence militant groups devoted to confronting non-Islamic cultures.

☙ CHRONOLOGY

1947
August: The subcontinent is partitioned; India incorporates West Bengal and Assam; Pakistan incorporates East Bengal (West Pakistan); Mohammed Ali Jinnah becomes the first governor-general of Pakistan; Liaquat Ali Khan becomes the first prime minister.
October: The first Indo-Pakistani war starts over Kashmir.

1948
September: Jinnah dies; Khawaja Nazimuddin becomes governor-general.

1949
January: The United Nations arranges a cease-fire between India and Pakistan.

1951
October: Liaquat Ali Khan is assassinated; Nazimuddin becomes prime minister; Ghulam Mohammed becomes governor-general.

1955
August: Ghulam Mohammed resigns; he is succeeded by Iskander Mirza.

1956
March: A constitution is adopted; Mirza becomes president.

1958
October: Mirza abrogates the constitution and declares martial law; Mirza is sent into exile; chief marshal law administrator (CMLA) General Mohammad Ayub Khan assumes the presidency.

1965
September: The second Indo-Pakistani war starts over Kashmir.

1969
March: Martial law is declared; Ayub Khan resigns; CMLA General Agha Mohammed Yahya Khan assumes the presidency.

1970

December: The first general elections are held; the Awami League under Mujib-ur-Rahman, and the Pakistan People's Party, under Zulfikar Ali Bhutto, emerge as the leading parties in East and West Pakistan, respectively.

1971

March: East Pakistan attempts to secede, beginning a civil war; Mujib is imprisoned in West Pakistan.

December: India invades East Pakistan; India recognizes Bangladesh; Yahya Khan resigns; Zulfikar Ali Bhutto becomes the CMLA and president.

1972

July: Bhutto and India's prime minister, Indira Gandhi, conclude the Simla Agreement, adjusting the 1949 cease-fire line, popularly known as the Line of Control.

1973

August: A new constitution goes into effect; Bhutto becomes prime minister.

1977

March: General elections are held; Bhutto's People's Party is blamed for rigging the elections; widespread rioting and protesting erupts.

July: Army Chief of Staff General Mohammad Zia-ul-Haq proclaims martial law and becomes the CMLA.

1978

September: Zia-ul-Haq becomes the nation's sixth president, replacing Fazal Ellahi Chaudry.

1979

April: Zulfikar Ali Bhutto is hanged as a result of a supreme court ruling in the murder case of Mohammed Qussory.

1988

May: President Zia-ul-Haq dismisses the government of Mohammed Khan Junejo, dissolves national and provincial assemblies, and orders a new election in ninety days.

August: Zia-ul-Haq, the U.S. ambassador to Pakistan, and top army officials are killed in an airplane crash near Bhawalpur in Punjab; Ghulam Ishaq Khan, chairman of the senate, is sworn in as the acting president.

December: Benazir Bhutto, leader of the Pakistan People's Party, emerges as the leader of the house and is sworn in as the first female prime minister of a Muslim nation.

1990

August: Benazir Bhutto is dismissed by President Ghulam Ishaq Khan for alleged corruption; Mian Nawaz Sharif succeeds her as the new prime minister.

1993

July: Sharif resigns along with President Ishaq Khan under an army-brokered agreement to end the bitter power tussle between the two top functionaries; after the election, Benazir Bhutto becomes the prime minister again.

1996

November: Benazir Bhutto is dismissed by President Farooq Ahmad Khan Leghari on misrule and corruption charges.

1997

February: The Pakistan Muslim League wins a sweeping election victory; Nawaz Sharif is appointed as prime minister and sets up an anticorruption unit.

1998

May: Relations with India deteriorate as the crisis in Kashmir deepens and Pakistan responds to India's first nuclear test by carrying out its own explosion in May.

1999

April: Bhutto and her husband are sentenced to five years in prison and are fined $8.6 million for alleged money laundering.

May: The Kargil Offensive against Indian forces in Kashmir begins.

October: Nawaz Sharif is ousted from power and is placed under house arrest after attempting to sack his army general Pervez Musharraf; Musharraf takes over as chief executive of Pakistan.

2000

May: The supreme court recognizes the Musharraf government and orders it to hold general elections by the end of 2002.

2001

June: Pervez Musharraf assumes the presidency under the Provisional Constitutional Order.

July: The Agra Summit is held between India and Pakistan in an effort to reduce tensions between the two South Asian powers.

October: A U.S. military operation against Afghanistan begins; Pakistan agrees to cooperate with the American war effort.

December: Tensions between India and Pakistan escalate after Islamic militants attack the Indian Parliament building in New Delhi.

2002

January: British prime minister Tony Blair visits Pakistan to reduce tensions between India and Pakistan; the South Asian Association for Regional Cooperation meets for the first time in three years in order to reduce tensions between India and Pakistan.

April: Pervez Musharraf holds a controversial referendum in which his presidency is extended through 2007.

October: Pakistan holds its first national elections since the military takeover of 1999; Musharraf reinstates the national assembly, provincial assemblies, and the national senate.

⚜ FOR FURTHER RESEARCH

Books

W. Norman Brown, *The United States and India, Pakistan, Bangladesh.* 3rd ed. Cambridge, MA: Harvard University Press, 1972.

Shahid Javed Burki, *Pakistan: Fifty Years of Nationhood.* 3rd ed. Boulder, CO: Westview Press, 1999.

Sumit Ganguly, *The Origins of War in South Asia: The Indo-Pakistani Conflicts Since 1947.* 2nd ed. Boulder, CO: Westview Press, 1994.

Sucheta Ghosh, *The Role of India in the Emergence of Bangladesh.* Calcutta: Minerva Associates, 1983.

Devin T. Hagerty, *The Consequences of Nuclear Proliferation: Lessons from South Asia.* Cambridge, MA: MIT Press, 1998.

H.V. Hodson, *The Great Divide: Britain, India, Pakistan.* New York: Atheneum, 1971.

J. Hussain, *A History of the Peoples of Pakistan: Towards Independence.* Karachi, Pakistan, and New York: Oxford University Press, 1997.

Ayesha Jalal, *The Sole Spokesman: Jinnah, the Muslim League, and the Demand for Pakistan.* Cambridge, England, and New York: Cambridge University Press, 1985.

Sheila McDonough, *Mohammed Ali Jinnah, Maker of Modern Pakistan.* Lexington, MA: Heath, 1970.

Allen Hayes Merriam, *Gandhi vs. Jinnah: The Debate over the Partition of India.* Columbia, MO: South Asia Books, 1980.

Mushtaqur Rahman, *Divided Kashmir: Old Problems, New Opportunities for India, Pakistan, and the Kashmiri People.* Boulder, CO: Lynne Rienner, 1996.

Kalim Siddiqui, *Conflict, Crisis, and War in Pakistan.* New York: Praeger, 1972.

Wayne Ayres Wilcox, *India and Pakistan.* New York: Foreign Policy Association, 1967.

Robert Wirsing, *India, Pakistan, and the Kashmir Dispute: On Regional Conflict and Its Resolution.* New York: St. Martin's Press, 1994.

Lawrence Ziring, *Pakistan in the Twentieth Century: A Political History.* Karachi, Pakistan, and New York: Oxford University Press, 1997.

Periodicals

Farhan Bokhari, "Why Pakistan Is a Launch Pad for Anti-U.S. Terrorists," *Christian Science Monitor,* November 14, 1997.

James Carney and John F. Dickerson, "Inside the War Room," *Time,* December 31, 2001.

Brahma Chellaney, "Fighting Terrorism in Southern Asia: The Lessons of History," *International Security,* December 2001.

Alexander Evans, "Talibanising Kashmir?" *World Today,* December 2001.

Sumit Ganguly, "India and Pakistan in the Shadow of Afghanistan," *Current History,* April 2002.

Seymour Hersh, "The Getaway," *New Yorker,* January 28, 2002.

———, "On the Nuclear Edge," *New Yorker,* March 23, 1993.

Tara Kartha, "Pakistan and the Taliban: Flux in an Old Relationship," *Strategic Analysis: A Monthly Journal of the ISDA*, October 2000. www.ciaonet.org.

Anatol Lieven, "The Pressures on Pakistan," *Foreign Affairs,* January/February 2002.

Rory McCarthy and Hasan Zaidi, "Can Pakistan Change?" *India Today International,* January 28, 2002.

Shaukat Qadir, "The Purpose of Deterrence Is to Deter," *Royal United Services Institute for Defense Studies,* April 2002.

Ahmed Rashid, "Pakistan, the Taliban, and the U.S.," *Nation,* October 8, 2001.

Marvin G. Weinbaum, "Pakistan and Afghanistan: The Strategic Relationship," *Asian Survey,* June 1991.

———, "War and Peace in Afghanistan: The Pakistani Role," *Middle East Journal,* Winter 1991.

Hasan Zaidi, "Between a Rock and a Hard Place," *India Today International,* January 14, 2002.

Websites

CIA, The World Fact Book: Pakistan, www.cia.gov. A site published by the American Central Intelligence Agency that provides extensive geographical and demographic information in addition to a basic overview of the structure of Pakistan's political institutions and economy.

Islamic Republic of Pakistan, www.pak.gov.pk. The official website of the Islamic Republic of Pakistan. This site offers links to current news items as well as features on the history and culture of Pakistan and the Kashmir conflict with India.

Pakistan: A Country Study, http://memory.loc.gov. This site is the online version of a book prepared by the Federal Research Division of the United States Library of Congress. Originally published in 1994, this site covers the historical development of Pakistan from the twenty-fifth century B.C. to the early 1990s and includes comprehensive information on social, political, and economic trends in Pakistan.

Pakistan Link, www.pakistanlink.com. A daily version of the Pakistani American periodical *Pakistan Link,* which publishes current news items and editorials and offers insight and analysis on the current affairs of Pakistan.

Pakistan Virtual Library, www.clas.ufl.edu. A subsection of the South Asia WWW Library that is supported by the College of Liberal Arts and Sciences at the University of Florida. This site is primarily a links page that provides access to a variety of pages including online periodicals, travel sites, and academic resource pages.

Story of Pakistan: The Website, www.storyofpakistan.com. Published by Jin Technologies Limited in Karachi, Pakistan, this site is one of the best resources on the Internet for the political history of Pakistan, covering the most prominent political leaders and the most important historical events from pre-history through independence.

▲ INDEX